CW01663633

AIP INDIAN FUSION

114 Autoimmune protocol compliant recipes with Indian flavors

Indira Pulliadath, MS, NTP

© 2020 Indira Pulliadath

All rights reserved. No part of this publication may be reproduced, distributed, or transmitted in any form or by any means, including photocopying, recording, or other electronic or mechanical methods, without the prior written permission of the publisher, except in the case of brief quotations embodied in critical reviews and certain other noncommercial uses permitted by copyright law.

Printed in the United States

ISBN: 978-1-7360978-0-9

AIP Indian Fusion is published by Cook2Nourish LLC in Glastonbury, Connecticut.

Photography by Indira Pulliadath
Book and Cover Design by Rachit Kumbalaparambil

Dedicated to my Amma and Acchan,
who inculcated in me the love for cooking

And thank you to my three darlings - my
husband and our two children, for making this
'labor of love' possible!

TABLE OF CONTENTS

FOREWORD

Autoimmune disease prevalence has increased dramatically in recent decades both in the USA and globally. Today, an estimated 50 million Americans, nearly 80 percent of whom are women, suffer from one or more autoimmune conditions.

The root cause of all autoimmune diseases is the same: our immune system mistakes a protein, cell or tissue in our own body for an invading pathogen, causing our immune systems to attack our own body with the same voracity normally reserved for an infectious organism like influenza. Which autoimmune disease a person develops is simply a matter of which protein, cell or tissue is mistakenly identified as foreign and thereby attacked by our immune system. For example, in Hashimoto's thyroiditis, the thyroid gland is attacked, while in rheumatoid arthritis, the tissues of our joints are attacked. While genetics account for about one-third of our risk for autoimmune disease, the rest comes from environmental exposures (infection, toxins and pollutants) and from poor diet and lifestyle.

The Autoimmune Protocol (abbreviated as AIP) is a framework for informing our day-to-day diet and lifestyle choices to support health and healing in the context of autoimmune and chronic illness. It is a complementary approach that can help to manage and even reverse the symptoms of autoimmune disease by providing the opportunity and nutritional resources required for immune regulation, gut health, hormone regulation and tissue healing.

The AIP diet focuses on nutrient density while avoiding processed and refined foods. The AIP also encourages sufficient sleep, stress management and activity as these are important lifestyle factors that are also immune modulators.

In recent years, medical studies have proven the effectiveness of AIP in reducing the symptoms of autoimmune disease. In a 2017 clinical trial in patients with Inflammatory Bowel Disease, 73% of participants achieved full clinical remission after following the protocol for only 6 weeks. A 2019 clinical trial in patients with Hashimoto's thyroiditis also showed improved quality of life in study participants after 10-weeks of AIP with the biggest improvements seen in physical functioning, energy, mental health and bodily pain.

While the AIP can be extremely effective, unfortunately, it also can be daunting. Even understanding the potential benefits of adopting the AIP, many folks still worry that they will have to give up all their comfort foods, that they might not get the support from their family, or that they may not be able to participate in gatherings with family and friends.

Indira also struggled with these same concerns, but she was so focused on reducing her pain and improving her quality of life that she dove headfirst into the AIP.

She quickly realized that the AIP was indeed reducing her inflammation, so she became determined to find a way to maintain 100% compliance until her body healed completely. Indira's pathway to sustaining the AIP included innovating in her kitchen to fuse the comforting flavors of her traditional Indian dishes with AIP dietary principles. And now, we all get to benefit from Indira's talent for recipe recreations!

Appropriately called AIP Indian Fusion, this cookbook features a fabulous collection of AIP-compliant recipes with an Indian twist—from appetizers, curries, stews and flatbreads to delectable desserts. You'll be inspired by new spices, novel cooking techniques and creative combinations of vegetables! With this cookbook, Indira has redefined what's possible in AIP comfort foods, gifting us all with an amazing resource to make us feel like we aren't missing out on anything while on the AIP!

- Dr. Sarah Ballantyne, PhD (aka The Paleo Mom) is an award-winning public speaker, New York Times bestselling author and world-renowned health expert.

INTRODUCTION

Ever since I learnt how to bake a cake in my high school 'Home Economics' class, I have been passionate about cooking. After I got married and moved to the United States from India, cooking began to hold a special meaning since I was trying to stay connected to my homeland by trying to cook my mom's recipes in my American kitchen. I was working full-time as a researcher and when I got home, cooking provided much needed stress relief!

I was diagnosed with Rheumatoid Arthritis in 2015. My symptoms started quite suddenly. I was working full-time and had a busy life cooking and taking care of our family of four and our home. One day suddenly while I was at work, I felt extremely fatigued and experienced severe pain on my left hip. I went home thinking it was probably a bad case of flu and then at night my right wrist started hurting. I took some Advil and went to sleep. But almost every other day after this I was having pains in some joint of my body. So I knew there was something seriously wrong. My pain flares kept coming and they kept getting worse and worse. One night I had such severe shoulder pain that my husband had to bring me to the emergency room. Painful episodes like these continued and finally after a period of 3 months, I got my RA diagnosis. The medications did not do much to reduce my pain flares and they also gave me scary side effects!

My breathing was affected and I had so much shortness of breath that I would gasp for air just climbing up the short flight of stairs in our house. After being on medications for over a year and not being able to handle the side effects, I decided to stop medications altogether. I went on disability from work and tried alternative therapies like naturopathy, ayurveda and homeopathy.

After quitting medications, my RA started progressing very fast. Within a period of 3 months, all my joints were affected. Even though I was trying to remain positive, I began to feel the pangs of frustration and hopelessness at times. And tears would flow when no one was around me. My condition began to decline further and pretty soon I could barely do anything around the kitchen. We hired part-time help to help me in the kitchen since I was unable to do the simplest of chores. Chopping vegetables for five minutes would make all my fingers swell up! Looking back, this period in my life was the lowest point in my journey. I love cooking and it made me depressed thinking that I might never be able to do much in the kitchen. I felt so depressed whenever I looked into the mirror since I didn't recognize the person staring back at me. It was very, very scary. The future looked bleak and I did not want to live a life where there was only pain and disability.

I wanted to do so much for my kids, had so many dreams and this was so not the future that I had foreseen for myself.

I continued researching on the internet for RA warriors who were doing better. I just could not resign myself to a life where I could not do all the things I loved to do like cooking and taking care of my family. Then one day one of my co-workers and a good friend was talking to me and she immediately sensed how acutely depressed I had become. She asked me if I was open to doing some meditation together and reading the Bible. I said yes instantly because I knew that I needed to have a spiritual connection to give me that positive energy that I was missing. And we started meeting every week. Within a few weeks of doing this, I started feeling positive again. I went from 'feeling sorry for myself' to feeling that there was hope and that God was trying to help me! I began praying with a fervor that I never had before.

Along with praying, I continued with my research and came across a naturopathic doctor from California who treated a lot of RA patients. I contacted her and she recommended the Paleo Autoimmune Protocol (AIP) to me. As I began to read Dr. Sarah Ballantyne's posts on the science behind the AIP, the 'science lover' in me was hooked. I had to definitely give it a try! I had started medications again and told my rheumatologist about the diet who wasn't very hopeful that it would help me. Before I started on AIP, my inflammation markers were very high (ESR was hovering around 50) despite being on medications. Within 3 months of being on AIP, my ESR dropped to within normal values shocking my rheumatologist!

So AIP definitely played a major role in my recovery. But what did it mean to eat AIP? Contrary to what some folks might think, eating 'AIP" does not mean that you will have nothing to eat! Although AIP is an elimination diet and you have to avoid a lot of foods, the focus of AIP is nutrient density. What this means is that you have to eat a lot of foods that are very high in nutrients. When you eliminate all potentially sensitive triggers (foods) and add in a variety of nutrient dense foods, you give the body a chance to heal itself. But no grains and just meat and vegetables? That's got to be boring, right? Wrong! That's where tapping into different cuisines came in handy for me! I was fortunate to be born in India raised by parents who originally hailed from Kerala, a coastal state in southern India. Seafood, plantains, coconuts, and root vegetables like cassava and taro root are staples in Keralan cuisine. I immediately noticed how it would be not too hard to create 'AIP Indian' dishes drawing inspiration from my southern Indian roots (pun intended!). After I embarked on AIP, I constantly looked into Keralan and other regional Indian cuisines to provide me inspiration. Having been cooking authentic Indian food as well as other international foods in my American kitchen for the past 20 years definitely helped! I soon realized that with a little bit of imagination, it was definitely possible to not only manage to stay on AIP but to also enjoy it! Having a burning desire to always cook a delicious meal, the past three years for me have been all about exploring and creating tasty Paleo and AIP meals by drawing in unique ingredients, flavors as well as techniques from Indian cuisine.

WHAT IS AIP?

The Autoimmune Protocol, abbreviated as AIP, is a powerful strategy that uses diet and lifestyle to help regulate the immune system and help the body heal from autoimmune disease. It is an elimination and reintroduction protocol that has been specifically designed to help those suffering from autoimmune disease determine their food allergies and sensitivities, reverse nutrient deficiencies, balance gut flora, and help regulate the immune system. This protocol is described in great detail by Dr. Sarah Ballantyne in her book, The Paleo Approach. The AIP diet focuses on two main things: eliminating inflammatory foods and adding nutrient dense foods. The goal of the Autoimmune Protocol is to power the body with healing nutrients while simultaneously avoiding inflammatory foods that might be contributing to disease. After initially eliminating all inflammatory foods for a period of time (up to 30 to 90 days), we can try to reintroduce some of the healthy foods back one food at a time observing our body carefully for any inflammation related symptoms.

What foods are to be avoided in the elimination phase of AIP?
During the elimination-phase of the Autoimmune Protocol, we need to exclude all grains, legumes, eggs, dairy, nuts, seeds, nightshade-family vegetables as well as food additives and chemicals from our diet. These foods have been shown in research to affect intestinal permeability leading to 'leaky gut' which has shown to be the root cause of autoimmunity. The removal of these foods can promote gut healing and balance the immune system.

See the table below for a detailed list of foods that need to be avoided:

Food Category	AIP Foods to avoid
Grains	Amaranth, Barley, Buckwheat, Bulgur, Corn Farro, Kamut, Millet, Oats, Quinoa, Rice, Rye, Sorghum, Spelt, Teff, Wheat
Nightshades	Ashwagandha, Bell Peppers, Cayenne, Chili Peppers, Eggplant, Habanero Peppers, Jalepeños, Paprika, Poblano Peppers, Potatoes, Sweet Pepper, Tobacco, Tomato, Tomatillo, Goji Berries (Wolf Berries)
Beans and Legumes	Adzuki Beans, Black Beans, Black-Eyed Peas, Chickpeas, Edamame, Fava Beans, Green Beans, Green Peas, Kidney Beans, Lentils, Lima Beans, Peanuts, Soybeans

Food Category	AIP Foods to avoid
Nuts and Seeds	Almond, Brazil Nuts, Cashew Nuts, Chestnut, Chia Seeds, Coffee, Cocoa/Chocolate, Flax Seeds, Hazelnut, Hemp Seeds, Macadamia Nuts, Pecan, Pine Nuts, Pistachio, Pumpkin Seeds, Sesame Seeds, Sunflower Seeds, Walnuts
Eggs and Dairy	Chicken Eggs, Duck Eggs, Goose Eggs, Butter, Cheese, Cream, Cream Cheese, Ghee, Milk, Yogurt
Spices	Allspice, Anise, Annatto, Caraway, Cardamom, Celery Seed, Coriander, Cumin, Fennel Seed, Fenugreek, Juniper, Mustard, Nutmeg, Pepper, Poppy
Alcohol	All Alcohol

What foods are to be included while doing the elimination phase of AIP?

The Autoimmune Protocol is not only about avoiding irritating trigger foods, but also about adding in nutrient-dense, whole foods that reverse micronutrient deficiencies, balance gut flora, and enable the body to heal. Some examples would be bone broth, organ meats, fermented foods, cold-water fish, shellfish, and a colorful array of fruits and vegetables.

See table below for a detailed list of AIP-allowed foods:

Food Category	AIP Allowed Foods
Vegetables	Artichoke, Arugula, Asparagus, Bok Choi, Broccoli, Brussels Sprouts, Cabbage, Cauliflower, Celery, Swiss Chard, Collard Greens, Green Cucumber, Fennel, Kale, Leek, Lettuce, Mushroom, Rhubarb, Snap Pea, Spinach, Squash, Watercress
Root vegetables	Beet, Turnip, Carrot, Radish, Celeriac Root, Rutabaga, Jicama, Shallot, Onion, Sweet Potato, Parsnip, Yam

Food Category	AIP Allowed Foods
Fruit	Apple, Apricot, Avocado, Banana, Blackberry, Blueberry, Cantaloupe, Cherry, Clementine, Coconut, Date, Fig, Grape, Grapefruit, Guava, Huckleberry, Honeydew, Kiwi, Mango, Nectarine, Peach, Plum, Strawberry, Watermelon
Meat	Beef, Bison, Buffalo, Lamb, Fish, Shellfish, Chicken, Turkey, Duck, Pork, Rabbit, Venison
Organ Meat (Offal)	Bone Broth, Liver, Kidney, Heart
Healthy Fats and Oils	Avocado Oil, Olive Oil, Coconut Oil, Palm Shortening, Lard, Beef Tallow, Duck fat, Bacon fat
Herbs	Basil, Bay Leaves, Chamomile, Chives, Cilantro, Dill, Lavender, Lemongrass, Marjoram, Mint, Parsley, Peppermint, Rosemary, Sage, Spearmint, Tarragon, Thyme
Spices	Asafoetida, Cinnamon, Cloves, Garlic, Ginger, Mace, Saffron, Sea Salt, Turmeric
Fermented vegetables	Fermented Cabbage (Sauerkraut), Fermented Vegetables (Carrot, Beet, Etc.), Beet Kvaas, Beet Kanji, Kombucha, Water Kefir
Pantry items	Apple Cider Vinegar, Baking Soda, Anchovies, Arrowroot Flour, Cassava Flour, Coconut Flour, Coconut Flakes, Coconut Vinegar, Coconut Aminos, Dates, Dried Fruit, Olives, Canned Salmon, Canned Sardines, Canned Tuna, Plantain Flour, Tigernut Flour, Ume Plum Vinegar, Tamarind

Source: autoimmunewellness.com

Reintroduction of Foods

As mentioned before, after strictly following the elimination phase of AIP for a period of time (anywhere between 30 to 90 days) and after you begin to feel better, you can start to reintroduce foods.

There are certain foods that you never want to reintroduce. Processed foods and gluten are an example of such foods. But there are a lot of the healthy foods that you can reintroduce. Dr. Sarah Ballantyne recommends the following order of reintroductions (see table on page 17) based on the nutrient density and the potential to cause or aggravate leaky gut.

The foods that are highly nutrient dense and have a low potential for stimulating the immune system are recommended to be reintroduced before the foods that are less nutrient dense and have a high tendency to cause leaky gut.

After following AIP elimination phase strictly for a couple months, I first reintroduced all the spices since I missed them the most. Now, I am able to tolerate even kashmiri red chilli peppers (stage 4 reintroduction) in small amounts. While all the recipes in this book are AIP elimination phase compliant, I have included suggested reintroduction notes (stage 1 and stage 2) for some of the recipes. But I suggest you follow the order of reintroductions as suggested by the table on page 17 and reintroduce foods slowly one food at a time so you can check if you react to it.

Stage 1 **Egg yolks (not the whites):** Chicken, duck, goose, quail, or any other type of egg yolk. **Legumes (beans with edible pods, and legume sprouts):** Green beans, peas, runner beans, snow peas, and sugar snap peas. **Fruit and berry-based spices:** Allspice, star anise, caraway, cardamom pod, juniper, pepper (from black, green, pink, or white peppercorns), and sumac. **Seed-based spices:** Anise seed, annatto seed, black caraway (Russian caraway, black cumin), celery seed, coriander seed, cumin seed, dill seed, fennel seed, fenugreek, mustard, and nutmeg. **Nuts and seeds (oils only):** Macadamia, sesame, and walnut. **Nuts and seeds:** Chocolate, cocoa, and coffee (occasional basis). **Dairy (ideally from grass-fed sources):** Ghee.
Stage 2 **Nuts and seeds:** Almonds, brazil nuts, cashews, chestnuts, coffee (daily basis), hazelnuts, macadamia nuts, pecans, pine nuts, pistachios, walnuts, chia, flax, hemp seeds, poppy, pumpkin seed, sesame, sunflower, or any other flavors, flours, butters, oils, and other products derived from them. **Egg whites (or whole eggs):** Chicken, duck, goose, quail, or any other type of egg white. **Dairy (ideally from grass-fed sources):** Butter and butter oil. **Alcohol (small quantities):** Gluten-free beer or hard cider (8 oz. or less), wine (5 oz. or less), fortified wine (3 oz. or less), liqueur (3 oz. or less), or gluten-free spirits (1 oz. or less).
Stage 3 **Nightshades (limited):** Bell peppers (aka sweet peppers), eggplant, paprika, and potatoes (peeled). **Dairy (ideally from grass-fed sources):** Buttermilk, cheese, cottage cheese, cream, cream cheese, curds, dairy-protein isolates, heavy cream, ice cream, kefir, milk, sour cream, whey, whey-protein isolate, whipping cream, and yogurt. **Legumes:** Chickpeas (aka garbanzo beans), lentils, and split peas. (Legumes may be more well tolerated when soaked and fermented).
Stage 4 **Nightshades or spices derived from nightshades:** Ashwagandha, cayenne peppers, cape gooseberries (aka ground cherries), garden huckleberries, goji berries (aka wolfberries), hot peppers (chili peppers and chili-based spices), naranjillas, pepinos, pimentos, potatoes (unpeeled), tamarillos, tomatillos, and tomatoes. **Gluten-free grains, pseudo-grains, and other grain-like substances:** Corn, fonio, Job's tears, millet, oats, rice, sorghum, teff, wild rice, amaranth, buckwheat, and quinoa (Grains may be more well-tolerated when soaked and fermented). **Legumes:** Adzuki beans, black beans, black-eyed peas, butter beans, calico beans, cannellini beans, fava beans (aka broad beans), Great Northern beans, Italian beans, kidney beans, lima beans, mung beans, navy beans, pinto beans, and peanuts. (Legumes may be more well tolerated when soaked and fermented). **Alcohol (moderate quantities):** Gluten-free beer or hard cider, wine, fortified wine, liqueur, or gluten-free spirits.

Source: thepaleomom.com

WHAT IS 'AIP INDIAN FUSION'?

Indian food is what I mostly ate for 26 years of my life. After my husband and I moved to the US, I started cooking it in my American kitchen. We also learned how to cook other cuisines and also learned to mix up different techniques and flavors. Of course, the predominant flavors in my kitchen have been Indian. So it was only natural that when I started on AIP, I would try to recreate AIP versions of Indian dishes! They were after all my comfort food and I knew in my heart that if I had to succeed on AIP, it was imperative that I improvise but yet create AIP versions of my favorite foods.

Over the last 3 years, I have tried and tested hundreds of recipes and quite a few of those made it to my blog. But there were also numerous ones that were created, noted on my phone but never made it to the blog just because I didn't have the time! And I kept telling myself that I would write an AIP cookbook including all of those recipes! Well, finally in the beginning of 2020, I decided that this was the year my first cookbook would be out!

As I started writing the book, I began to wonder what title to give it. 'Indian Inspired AIP' definitely came to mind. However, most, if not all, of the recipes seemed as if they were created by blending different flavors, spices, cuisines and cooking techniques. Something old, Something new, Something borrowed and Something blue! Tandoori Chicken Pizza, Green Chutney Baked Fish, Kerala Beef Bowl, Chicken Paapdi Chaat, and Mango Pie are some examples of what you will find in this book. All of them do have an Indian element but the recipes are greatly influenced by other international dishes/cuisines too. So clearly there was some fusion going on there. Plus, when I decided to write this book and was trying out recipes, many times I was taking an existing recipe that was actually 'my modified version' of the traditional Indian recipe to begin with, and then subjecting it to further modifications so as to fit the AIP criteria! Hence 'AIP Indian Fusion' seemed like a perfect way to describe this book! It is a fusion of AIP with Indian and a fusion of Indian and AIP with a whole lot of other culinary influences. I honestly feel that the book is a fusion and an explosion of flavors and a perfect example of the current food scene worldwide, which is an amalgamation of different foods, cultures and regions.

One of the great things about Indian food is that a lot of spices go into a dish. Every Indian dish has anywhere between 5 to 10 different spices. But the beauty lies in the proportions of those spices. So two curries with the same 5 spices can still taste very different and that would be because of the different ratio of the spices in each of those recipes.

In AIP, since many spices need to be eliminated, I took it as a challenge to still combine the allowed spices in different ways so that I could still create different curry options for myself. And that is something you will see in the recipes in this book a lot – me playing with the flavors!

AIP has helped me tremendously in improving my quality of life and so I really want to recommend this incredibly healing diet to all those who are suffering from an autoimmune disease. One of my goals in creating this book was to make AIP more appealing so that more and more folks feel encouraged to try this diet! There are many people who hear about AIP but feel challenged to do the diet because they are afraid of feeling deprived. That is one thing I really want to help change. When I first finished writing this entire book, I felt really satisfied and joyful. I could not believe how many recipes I had been creating these past few years! I am really hopeful that many folks would feel tempted to not only try AIP but also stick to it owing to the delicious recipes in this book!

I sincerely hope that you enjoy this book as much as I have enjoyed creating it! And may the AIP diet heal you and bring much joy into your life.

There is now a lot of evidence that AIP works. Scores of testimonials from people suffering from various autoimmune diseases as well as recent medical studies have proven that. My desire in writing this book is to show you that AIP does not have to be boring! In fact I really believe that you can have your curry and eat it too!

Curry Leaves Plant

SHOPPING FOR SPECIAL INGREDIENTS

Until a couple of years ago, shopping for any exotic spices or any special pantry ingredients was very hard and limited to the respective ethnic local supermarket. Nowadays, Amazon and other online shops have made it really easy to shop online for different spices and specialty ingredients that otherwise would have been challenging to find in regular grocery stores. The prices are also usually competitive since there are usually more than one seller. For the recipes in this book, I have created a table below showing different places where you can buy them including some notes to help you shop for them. I have also included my preferred brand for them wherever applicable. I have also included a column to show you alternative ingredients if you cannot find the ingredient of choice mentioned in the recipe.

Ingredient Name (Indian Name)	Description/ Characteristics to Look for	Recommended Brands (where to find them)	Alternates/ Substitutes
Aamchur (Dried Mango powder)	Available in powder or dried pieces. It is used as a souring agent in spice blends and in curries. Make sure the product is gluten free.	Indian grocers and amazon.com. Double check label to ensure product is gluten free and free of any other additives	Tart Fresh or frozen Green Mango, Lime juice
Anchovies	Fresh frozen anchovies are what works best and the tiny bones can be eaten as well!	Indian or Asian grocery stores	If you can't find fresh frozen anchovies, you can get canned ones (Wild Planet brand) too that are available online on Thrive or in other health stores.

Ingredient Name (Indian Name)	Characteristics to look for	Recommended Brands (where to find them)	Alternates/ Substitutes
Asafoetida	Available in powder or rock form. Powdered form in a convenient dispenser is recommended for ease of use; Make sure the product is gluten free.	Indian grocers and amazon.com.	None
Coconut Milk	Homemade using frozen fresh grated coconut (mentioned below) or canned organic coconut milk, unsweetened and without any additives or thickeners.	Aroy-D, Native Forest Simple (Whole Foods, Trader Joe's, Regular Grocers, Amazon.com)	Coconut Milk powder (check ingredients to make sure it is AIP compliant)
Cassava (Yuca)	Cassava also called as yuca or manioc is the starchy tuberous root of a tree grown in tropical countries like Brazil, Africa and southern India. The roots can be cooked (after peeling them) and are a good source of complex carbs in a grain free diet	American grocers in the International section, International grocers	If you cannot find fresh cassava root, look for frozen cassava in the frozen vegetables aisle.

Ingredient Name (Indian Name)	Characteristics to look for	Recommended Brands (where to find them)	Alternates/ Substitutes
Cassava Flour	Cassava flour is prepared from cassava root and it is great for making grain free flatbreads and in baking.	Otto's (Whole Foods, amazon.com), Anthony's Goods (amazon.com)	None—I don't recommend any other brands because their quality is unpredictable.
Dried Ginger powder (Ground ginger)	Fresh Ginger root is very widely used in Indian cuisine and is a must in most curries! Dried ginger powder has a longer shelf-life and hence is useful when fresh root is not available. Dried ginger is also particularly useful for making teas and in desserts and baked goods like cookies where the ginger taste does not get too overpowering. In India, dried ginger is called as 'sonth' and is used in most ayurvedic medicines too because of its digestive and anti-inflammatory qualities.	Whole Foods, Indian grocers, amazon.com	Fresh ginger root
Dried Rose petals	Dried rose petals are used in Indian and Middle Eastern cuisine mainly in teas or in desserts for a floral flavor. Make sure to purchase only an organic, food grade product. These can be infused into teas or to make an extract or even powdered and added to dishes.	Indian or Middle Eastern grocers, amazon.com	Rose water, Rose extract

Ingredient Name (Indian Name)	Characteristics to look for	Recommended Brands (where to find them)	Alternates/ Substitutes
Extra Virgin Coconut Oil	Unrefined, cold pressed extra virgin coconut oil has rich flavor and aroma and that is what's used traditionally in southern Indian cooking. It has a smoke point of 350 F so avoid using it for deep frying but it is great for moderate heat cooking like sauteing. In many curry recipes, extra virgin coconut oil is drizzled over the top in the end after the curry is done cooking.	Whole Foods and other American grocers, amazon.com	Refined coconut oil can be used if you don't like the strong flavor and aroma of coconut.
Fresh Curry Leaves	Leaves should be fresh vibrant green with no or minimal black spots. These are usually in a sealed plastic pouch and are priced around $2 for each package which contains 6-8 sprigs of leaves.	Indian grocery stores in the 'fresh herbs' section – Some stores will also store these separately and you may need to inquire with store personnel to locate them; Some sellers also sell fresh curry leaves on amazon.com but the price would be at least 4-5 times as compared to the Indian grocery store.	Dried curry leaves (available in Indian grocery stores or on amazon.com); However, dried curry leaves do not have the same flavor as fresh curry leaves so use them only if you do not have an Indian grocer in your area!
Fresh Fenugreek leaves	Fenugreek leaves called as methi leaves are used widely in Indian cuisine in flatbreads and also in vegetable side dishes or even added to meat dishes for the flavor. Fenugreek leaves are also very medicinal in nature and are excellent for digestion and also useful in lowering blood glucose, cholesterol as well as improving lactation in breast feeding women.	Indian grocers	Dried fenugreek leaves

Ingredient Name (Indian Name)	Characteristics to look for	Recommended Brands (where to find them)	Alternates/ Substitutes
Frozen Fresh Grated Coconut	Grated when fresh and then frozen; on thawing the product should be very close to freshly grated coconut with no rancid smell	Daily Delight, Deep foods (Indian grocery stores in the frozen vegetables section)	Organic unsweetened dried Shredded coconut – Bob's Red Mill, Nature's Promise
Ginger garlic paste	Ginger garlic paste is used a lot in Indian curries and I always like to use fresh home made ginger garlic paste. However, if you are in a rush, store bought ginger garlic paste can definitely come handy! Make sure you get an organic brand that doesn't contain any non AIP ingredients.	Indian grocers, amazon.com	Home made fresh ginger garlic paste or sub just finely chopped fresh ginger and garlic.
Kala Namak (Black Salt)	Kala Namak, also known as Black Salt, is used widely in Indian cuisine. It is pinkish grey rather than black and has a very distinctive sulfurous mineral taste similar to hard-boiled eggs. This Black Salt is used as a condiment and is added to chaat masala, chutneys, raitas and many other savory Indian snacks.	Indian or Pakistani grocers, amazon.com	None really as this has an unique flavor; however you can just substitute pink himalayan salt or any sea salt.

Ingredient Name (Indian Name)	Characteristics to look for	Recommended Brands (where to find them)	Alternates/ Substitutes
Kasoori Methi (Dried Fenugreek leaves)	The leaves have a strong, 'not so pleasant' smell and come in packs larger than your typical spice packets because of the high volume of the dried leaves.	MDH / Swad (Indian grocery stores, amazon.com)	Fresh fenugreek leaves (Indian grocery stores in the 'fresh herbs' section)
Kudampuli (Malabar tamarind)	Dried fruit pieces which are black in color are packaged ; There may be specks of coarse sea salt and some sand which is ok	Indian grocers and amazon.com.	Tamarind extract or regular tamarind both of which can be found at Indian grocers or on amazon.com
Okra	Okra, also called as 'Ladies finger' in many countries is a mucigenous vegetable. When shopping, look for firm, springy pods about 2-3 inches long. The smaller, tender ones have the best texture when cooked.	Indian grocers (under both fresh produce and frozen vegetables section) and regular grocers (frozen vegetables section)	None
Plantains	Plantains belong to the banana family but are starchier and less sweet than bananas. Both green (unripe) and yellow (ripe plantains) are used in southern Indian cooking. Unlike bananas, plantains need to be cooked before consumption.	Indian, Asian and other ethnic grocers and regular grocers.	Green bananas can be a substitute for green plantains. And regular banana can be a substitute for ripe plantain in some recipes.

Ingredient Name (Indian Name)	Characteristics to look for	Recommended Brands (where to find them)	Alternates/ Substitutes
Rose water	Rose water is a floral water made by distilling or simmering rose petals. It's often used in Middle Eastern, Persian, and Indian cooking. In India, it is primarily used in sweet dishes like gulab jamun and kheer. Rose water has a very distinct flavor and it's an absolutely wonderful addition to many dishes when used in moderation.	Whole Foods, Indian or Middle Eastern grocers, (Cortas) amazon.com	Rose extract
Saffron	Has a potent aroma and a little goes a long way. Look for pure quality organic saffron without any additives or colorants	Indian grocers and amazon.com	None
Sliced Coconut	Sliced coconut is used very commonly in southern Indian cuisine both in vegetable side dishes and in meat dishes. You can eat either fresh coconut slices (from a fresh coconut) or get fresh frozen coconut slices.	Indian or Asian grocery stores	Dried coconut slices

Ingredient Name (Indian Name)	Characteristics to look for	Recommended Brands (where to find them)	Alternates/ Substitutes
Stone flower (Dagad Phool or Kalpasi)	The texture of this spice is paper like and when raw it has a very faint smell	Indian grocers and amazon.com. Double check label to ensure product free of any other additives	None
Tapioca flour	Tapioca starch is also obtained from cassava root (just like cassava flour) however it is more processed to isolate only the starch and does not include the fiber from the root.	Bob's Red Mill (American grocers, Whole Foods, amazon.com)	Arrowroot starch works as a good substitute for tapioca flour in most recipes
Tapioca Pearls (Sabudana)	Tapioca pearls are round pellets made from cassava roots and in India are mainly used during periods of religious fasting. The variety used in Indian cuisine are white in color and are large (#40 size). Before using these pearls in a recipe, they must be soaked overnight or for at least 2 hours.	Indian grocers, amazon.com	None
Tiger nuts	Tiger nuts, also known as chufa, are not actually nuts, but rather edible tubers. They're the size of a chickpea but wrinkly with a chewy texture and sweet nutty flavor similar to coconut. They are great in baking and in desserts! Soaking them for 6-8 hours improves their taste and texture.	Amazon.com or other online health food stores	No AIP substitute

Ingredient Name (Indian Name)	Characteristics to look for	Recommended Brands (where to find them)	Alternates/ Substitutes
Tiger nut flour	Tiger nut flour is obtained by grinding tigernuts which are tubers. This flour is a great grain free option for baking as it has a rich nutty taste.	Gemini, Anthony's Goods (Health food stores, Amazon.com)	No AIP substitute
Water Chestnut Flour (Singhada Atta or Singoda Atta)	The flour is ground from dried ground water chestnuts. For preparing the flour, the nuts are peeled, boiled and finally crushed into flour. Singhada flour is used in India in a lot of communities during periods of religious fasting where grains and legumes are not consumed.	Indian grocers, amazon.com	For some recipes, tigernut flour can be a good substitute.
White Sweet Potato	Purple Skinned sweet potato with white flesh on the inside	Indian or Asian grocery stores; Whole Foods and other American grocers	Japanese Sweet potato is similar to this so you can substitute with that; Substitution with regular orange sweet potato may be possible in some recipes and is noted wherever appropriate.

- RECIPES -

Cooking Basics

Recipe Abbreviations
tsp - teaspoon
tbsp - tablespoon
lb = pound (~ 0.4536 kg)

Special kitchen appliances and tools I recommend:
Food processor, Blender, Instant Pot, Rolling pin, Peeler, Box Grater, Colander/Strainer, Zester, Immersion Blender, Potato Masher, Mandolin Slicer, Spiralizer, Nut Milk Bag

Pots and pans: My favorite type of cookware is stainless steel. I also like to use cast iron pans.

For baking, I like to use parchment sheet lined non stick or metal baking pans. For higher temperatures, I use aluminium foil but I try to limit the use of Aluminium.

Oven temperatures:
Oven temperatures vary greatly across different types and brands of ovens so a range is provided usually for the oven times. Always check for doneness of a recipe at the lower end of the time range.

Now that you know what foods are allowed on AIP and what foods should be avoided, you are probably wondering what your meals will look like. If you have been eating a lot of grains and legumes, then initially it can seem daunting. However, once you focus on the foods that you can eat, you will find that there are indeed a lot of options!

In general, I recommend to my clients that they focus on eating three full and balanced meals a day initially. A balanced meal means that your plate should comprise of 30-40% carbs (coming from vegetables and starchy vegetables), 30% protein and 30-40% fats. Staying within these macronutrient ratios will help you to feel satiated between meals and will curb cravings. In the first couple weeks, you are likely to feel symptoms of low blood sugar and detox which include fatigue, headaches and low energy. As you continue to stay on the diet, these symptoms will resolve and you will slowly begin to see increased energy levels. I highly recommend consuming Bone Broth regularly (at least 3 to 5 times per week) in the first few weeks of AIP.

The recipes in this book have been categorized into sections for ease of choosing a recipe. Most of the recipes under 'Satisfying' as well as those under 'Curryto Bowls' can be full meals on their own. For all the other recipes, I mention how I pair them with other sides (salad, vegetable sides or breads) to make a complete meal. And you can totally create your own combinations!

Before I started AIP, I used to think that the key to making a fantastic curry dish was in using a variety of spices. But while doing AIP I realized that wasn't necessarily true. Sometimes using fewer spices in the right proportions can make not only those individual flavors stand out but also elevates a simple dish to great heights!

All the recipes are 100% Elimination AIP compliant. However, I have included 'reintroduction notes' in some recipes that you can use to enhance the recipes as you start reintroducing foods some of the foods back.

TEMPTING

As the name suggests, 'Tempting' stands for appetizing small bites and are great combined with salads. Some of these are great for batch cooking, for example, Chicken Shaami Kebabs, Sardine Cutlets, Curried Beef and Chicken Liver Masala. You can make a big batch over the weekend and then throughout the week you can have them for lunch paired with a small salad or any vegetable side.

Some of them, like Crispy Chicken Bites and Fish Pakoras, taste best when made closer to the meal time. However, as long as the chicken or fish is thawed in advance, they do not take too much time to prep and cook!

Chicken Paapdi Chaat is my favorite one from this category and can be rustled up pretty quickly! Do not let the length of the recipe intimidate you! This can be a full meal in itself or you could make it as an appetizer and serve in smaller portions when you are entertaining!

The Kheema Samosas do take up time however they will be worth all your time and efforts as they are so delicious! If you plan to make a big batch of this for a party, try to get a friend or a family member to help you to assemble the samosas as it can be tiresome!

Fish Pakoras

These crispy fish fritters are scrumptious and have a ton of flavor! The traditional 'pakora' batter uses chickpea flour however, cassava flour works great in this recipe! Paired with a salad, it makes a filling meal!

Serves 2

Ingredients:

For marinating the fish:
A generous bunch of fresh cilantro leaves (about 1/2 a cup)
1 large garlic clove (or two small cloves), peeled
1 inch by 1/2 inch piece of fresh ginger, peeled
1/4 tsp sea salt
2 tsp water
About 4 flounder filet pieces or any other white fish each about 4 oz, cut into 1 inch by 2 inch pieces

For the batter:
1/4 cup Otto's cassava flour
1/4 tsp sea salt
1/4 tsp turmeric
1/4 cup plus 2 tsp water
1 tbsp finely chopped fresh cilantro
Coconut oil for shallow frying, about 4 tbsp

Reintroduction Notes: *You can add 1/4 tsp whole cumin seeds or ground cumin (which is a stage 1 reintroduction) to the batter for additional flavor.*

Method:

In a small food processor jar, grind the cilantro, garlic, ginger, sea salt and water. (It's ok if the mixture is somewhat chunky - A small food processor jar like Magic Bullet works best. You can also use a mortar and pestle). Keep aside.

In a medium size mixing bowl, place the fish pieces. Dab them using a paper towel to get rid of excess moisture. Then add the marinade to this bowl and using your hands coat each fish piece with the marinade. Keep aside.
In another mixing bowl, add all the batter ingredients and mix using a fork or a whisk to get a smooth mixture. Mixture will be quite thick.

Heat a stainless steel or non stick frying pan on medium heat for about 3-4 minutes until it is hot and then add about 2 tbsp of coconut oil to it and let heat for about 1 minute until the oil is hot.

Now add about 6-8 pieces of fish to the batter bowl and then one by one take each piece of coated fish and place on the pan. Shallow fry the fish on medium heat for about 2 minutes and then flip and cook for 2 more minutes on the other side until you get a crispy golden color on both sides. Transfer to a plate lined with paper towels.

Repeat process with remaining fish.
Serve the pakoras hot as they will lose their crispiness upon cooling.

Crispy Chicken Bites

Crispy sweet and spicy chicken bites with the flavors of ginger and garlic! These are perfect as an appetizer or can be paired with a salad for a delicious meal!

Serves: 3-4

Ingredients:
1 lb. chicken pieces, boneless thigh pieces, cut into bite size pieces

Marinade:
3⁄4 tsp sea salt
1 1⁄2 tbsp fresh ginger and garlic paste (see recipe for ginger garlic paste on page 220)
2 tsp coconut aminos
1 tbsp cassava flour plus 1 tbsp tapioca flour/starch

About 1/4 cup coconut oil for shallow (pan) frying

Method:

In a large bowl, add the chicken pieces and blot dry using paper towels.
Add the salt, ginger garlic paste and the coconut aminos to the chicken and mix using your hands to coat the chicken well.
Sprinkle the cassava flour and the tapioca starch on top. Again mix using your hands to coat the chicken pieces completely.

Heat a skillet and when hot, about 2 tbsp oil to it. When the oil gets hot, drop the chicken pieces one by one using a spoon or your hands. Pan fry (shallow fry) them in batches on medium heat until they are cooked well and crispy on both sides, about 2 minutes on each side (The oil can splutter a lot while the chicken is frying so stay away from the pan). Drain on paper towels and serve hot!

Notes: I like to use a stainless steel skillet for pan frying and use a fork to flip the pieces.

Reintroduction Notes:
You can add half a teaspoon of ground black pepper (stage 1 reintroduction) in the marinade.

Sardine Cutlets

I love sardines in any form - pan fried or curried ! These cutlets or patties are great for those of you who are not great fans of sardines as the veggies and spices mask the strong taste. This recipe works well with any other fish as well.

Serves 2-3

Ingredients:

2 cans sardines in oil or water (about 4 oz each)
1 tbsp coconut oil
1/2 of a medium red onion, chopped fine
1 tbsp finely chopped garlic
1 tsp finely chopped (or grated) fresh ginger or 1 tsp ground ginger
3/4 tsp turmeric
1/4 tsp sea salt
1 tsp ground cinnamon
2 cups grated zucchini (about 1 medium size zucchini)
1/4 cup cassava flour
1 tsp Aamchur (dried mango powder) or 1 tbsp lemon juice
1/4 cup finely chopped fresh cilantro leaves
about 1/4 cup coconut oil for pan frying

Method:

Drain the water or oil from the sardines by using a strainer. Place the sardines in a large mixing bowl. Mash it with a fork and keep aside.

Heat a sauté pan and add the coconut oil. When the oil gets hot, add the onions. Saute on medium for about 2 minutes and then add the ginger and garlic. Sauté for 30 seconds and then add the turmeric, salt and the cinnamon. Stir to mix and turn heat off. Let cool.

Place the grated zucchini on a clean dish cloth or muslin cloth and squeeze it to get the water out of it as much as possible. Discard the water and add the zucchini into the bowl with the sardines.

Now add the onion and spice mixture also into the bowl. Also add the cassava flour, the aamchur (or the lemon juice) and the cilantro.

Using your hands, mix everything together well and then divide the mixture into 6 equal portions. Take each portion and make a patty by shaping with your hands. Place each patty on a plate.

Heat a frying pan or sauté pan. Add 1/2 of the coconut oil for frying. Let heat for 2 minutes and then turn heat to medium. Add 3-4 patties into the pan one by one and cook for about 3 minutes on each side. Flip carefully using a spatula and again cook for about 2 minutes on the other side. Transfer to a plate. Add the rest of the oil to the pan and finish frying the rest of the patties the same way.

Recipe on next page

Kheema Samosas

It took me multiple recipes and many weekends to perfect this samosa recipe! Instead of the traditional potatoes and pea stuffing, I use a spiced ground chicken stuffing which makes these irresistible!

Serves: 4-8 (makes 16 samosas)

Ingredients:

For the filling:
2 tbsp olive oil or coconut oil
1/2 of a medium red onion, chopped fine
1 tbsp grated fresh ginger
1 tbsp chopped fresh garlic
1/2 tsp turmeric
1/2 tsp sea salt
1/2 tsp ground cinnamon
1 lb. ground chicken, thawed
2 tbsp finely chopped fresh cilantro
2 tbsp shredded coconut

For the covering:
3/4 cup cassava flour
1/4 cup arrow root flour
1/2 tsp sea salt
1 tbsp olive oil
1 cup hot water (that has been boiling)
extra 1-2 tsp olive oil

For deep frying:
About 2 cups palm shortening or avocado oil

Method:

To make the filling:
Heat a large sauté pan and when hot lower the heat and add the oil. Then add the onion and sauté for 2 minutes on medium heat. Then add the ginger and garlic. Saute for 1 more minute. Then add the salt and the spices.

Stir fry for another 30 seconds and then add the ground chicken. Let cook for 2-3 minutes and then using a wooden spatula, move the chicken around so as to get it cooked fully from all sides. As the chicken cooks, it will let out water. So when that happens, push the chicken to the sides of the pan and let the water concentrate in the middle.

Turn heat to low and let the water evaporate completely. It will take about 8-10 minutes. When all the water is gone, add the cilantro and the coconut. Stir to mix well and turn heat off. Let this filling mixture cool completely (15-20 mins) before making the samosas.

To make the covering:
In a large mixing bowl, add the flours, salt and the olive oil. Then add the hot water slowly stirring as you add the water. Make sure all the flour is mixed and there is no dry flour.

Let the dough cool for a couple minutes and then using your hands knead the now warm dough. Add the extra oil if needed to make the dough smooth and non sticky. Divide the dough into 8 equal balls.

To make the samosas:
Place a deep skillet (or small wok style pan) with the oil for heating for deep frying the samosas.

While the oil is getting hot, you can start making the samosas.

Roll each dough ball into a circle (about 4 inches in diameter). Then using a pizza cutter or a knife, cut the circle into two semi-circles.

Take each semi-circle and shape into a cone shape pressing the straight edges together with a little bit of water. Then take 1 tbsp of the now cooled filling mixture and carefully place inside the cavity (of the cone) and seal the edges using some more water.

Place on a tray. Repeat the process with the other semi-circle. And then repeat the same process with all the rest of the dough balls. You will have 16 samosas.

When the oil turns hot, turn the heat to low medium (number 6) and wait for a couple minutes and then start frying the samosas 2-4 at a time depending upon how big your skillet is.
Fry them for about 2 minutes on one side and flip and fry for 2 minutes on that side and flip again and fry for 1 more minute until golden brown and crispy. Repeat for all the rest of the samosas.

Chicken Shaami Kebabs

These kebabs were one of the first AIP recipes I created and are so versatile! You can make a large batch and freeze them. And have with salad, as a lettuce burger or in tacos!

Serves: 4-5

Ingredients:

1 lb organic ground chicken, thawed completely at room temperature
1/2 of a medium size red onion, finely chopped
2 tbsp finely chopped fresh ginger (about 2 inch by 2 inch piece)
2 tbsp finely chopped garlic (about 8-10 cloves)
1 cup packed fresh cilantro leaves, finely chopped
3/4 tsp sea salt
1/2 tsp turmeric powder
1 tsp dry mango powder (aamchur)
1 tsp dried fenugreek leaves (kasoori methi)
1 tsp lime or lemon juice
2 tbsp extra virgin olive oil

About 3/4 cup coconut oil for shallow frying or grilling

Method:

Take the ground chicken in a large mixing bowl. (Make sure it is completely thawed and make sure to dab dry with paper towel to remove any excess water)

Next add all the other ingredients including the extra virgin olive oil into the bowl with the chicken. (Make sure you have chopped everything really fine)

Then using a spatula or your hands mix the chicken with all the spices and the other ingredients so that it is uniformly mixed.

Heat a large frying pan with about 2 tbsp of the coconut oil (for shallow frying) and make about 1 inch thick rounded patties of the ground mixture.

Cook on medium heat for about 2 minutes on one side and then flipping them to cook on the other side for an additional 2 minutes or so. (Make sure you do not overcook them or they will get hard and dry!) Remove onto a plate lined with paper towel to drain off excess oil.

Curried Beef With Coconut Chips

This is a traditional Keralan recipe where I have omitted the non-AIP spices. The ginger, garlic ,sliced coconuts, fresh curry leaves and the extra virgin coconut oil give this dish so many depths of flavor!

Serves: 3-4

Ingredients:
1 lb. grass fed beef (stew meat or flank steak), cut into 1 inch cubes
1/2 tsp sea salt
1 tsp turmeric
2 tbsp fresh grated ginger
2 whole cloves
1 inch cinnamon stick
1 bay leaf
1 tbsp extra virgin coconut oil

For the garnish:
2 tbsp extra virgin coconut oil
1/2 cup fresh frozen coconut slices that have been thawed to room temperature (or coconut chips)
1/4 cup shallot or red onion, finely chopped
1 tbsp garlic, finely chopped
8-10 fresh curry leaves (or dried curry leaves)

Method:

In a medium size heavy bottomed cooking pot, place the beef pieces. Blot dry using paper towels. Then add the salt, the turmeric, the ginger, the whole spices and the coconut oil. Using your hands mix all the spices well with the meat.

Cover the pot with a tight fitting lid and place the pot to heat on low heat for about 15-20 minutes stirring occasionally to avoid scorching. (Alternatively you can also pressure cook the meat in an Instant Pot for 7 minutes releasing pressure naturally.)

Turn heat off and transfer the cooked beef pieces into a plate leaving out the whole spices. (The beef would have let out water which would make a great stock so reserve that stock for later)

For the garnish:
Heat a skillet and add the coconut oil. When hot, turn heat to medium and add the coconut slices(or the chips) and toast for about 2-3 minutes until they begin to turn golden brown.

Remove them using a slotted spoon and transfer them onto the plate with the cooked beef.

To the same skillet, add the onions, garlic and the curry leaves. Saute on medium heat stirring continuously until the onions turn golden brown and crisp. Now add the beef and coconut mixture to the skillet and stir fry for a couple minutes to coat the meat well. Transfer to a serving dish and serve warm!

Chicken, Okra and Mushroom Stir Fry

The beauty of this dish is in its simplicity. The combination of okra with mushrooms is really wonderful because of the different textures. And then when you add chicken into the mix, it becomes even more delightful!

Serves 2 (as a meal) or 4 (served with cassava rotis)

Ingredients:

1 lb. chicken thigh or chicken breast pieces, cut into 1 inch cubes
1/2 tsp sea salt
1/4 tsp turmeric
2 -3 tbsp coconut oil (or avocado oil)
1 medium red onion, thinly sliced
4-6 fresh curry leaves
1 tsp fresh ginger minced or grated
1 cup sliced okra (fresh or frozen)
1/8 tsp sea salt
1 cup sliced mushrooms
1 tsp lime juice (optional)

Method:

In a large mixing bowl, add the chicken pieces and dab dry with paper towels to get the extra moisture out. Sprinkle with the sea salt and turmeric and using your hands coat the chicken pieces well. Set aside.

Heat a large stainless steel pan and when hot, add about 2 tbsp of the oil. When the oil is hot, turn heat to medium and add the chicken pieces and shallow fry them in the oil (depending upon the size of your pan, you may need to do this in batches).

Cook the chicken pieces on each side for about 3 minutes on medium heat and then flip and cook for another 2 minutes. Transfer to a dish and keep aside along with any juices.

To the same pan, add the rest of the coconut oil and when hot add the onions and curry leaves and stir fry for about 2 minutes till soft. Next, add the salt and the ginger and stir fry for 30 seconds.

Then add the okra pieces and cook for 3-4 minutes (longer if using frozen okra) until the okra gets crisp. Cover and cook for 2 minutes. Add the mushrooms next and stir fry for another two minutes until they are cooked.

Add the chicken back to the same pan along with its juice and stir fry everything together for two more minutes. Take care not to stir the okra too much as it can get mushed.
Serve warm as is or with cassava rotis!

Chicken Papdi Chaat

Chaat is 'Indian street food' and as kids, the very mention of it would get our mouths watering! Chaat essentially comprises of a mix of some fried foods, some starchy foods like potatoes, peas or chickpeas mixed with an array of tantalizing spicy, sweet and tangy chutneys!

Serves 4

Ingredients:

1 lb. boneless chicken thighs or breasts
1/2 tsp sea salt
1 inch by 2 inch piece of fresh ginger, thinly sliced or grated (about 2 tbsp)
1/2 cup water
4 Homemade cassava tortillas (see recipe on page 159) (or you can use store bought AIP compliant tortillas)
About 1 1/2 cups avocado oil for deep frying

For assembling the chaat:
1 large white sweet potato, boiled, peeled and cut into 1/2 inch cubes
2 tsp chaat masala (see recipe on page 224)
2 tbsp finely chopped red onion
2 tbsp finely chopped fresh cilantro leaves
1/2 cup of pomegranate arils
About 4-5 tbsps of tamarind chutney (see recipe on page 208)
About 4-5 tbsps of cilantro coconut chutney (see recipe on page 205)

Method:

In a medium size cooking pot, add the chicken, the salt, ginger and water. Heat till the water comes to a boil and then cover and cook on low heat for about 15 minutes till the meat is cooked through. Turn heat off and let cool for sometime before shredding the chicken.

Reserve the chicken stock and divide the shredded chicken into 4 servings and keep aside. Divide the sweet potato cubes into 4 equal servings and keep aside.

For making the papdis:
Heat the oil for frying in a deep frying pan. Cut the tortillas into 2 inch by 1/2 inch strips. If using homemade ones that were refrigerated, make sure they come to room temperature first before frying them.

Deep fry the tortilla strips on medium heat for about 2 minutes until they turn golden brown (take care not to burn them). Remove from the oil using a slotted spoon and drain on paper towels to remove excess oil.

Alternately, you can also brush the tortilla strips with oil and bake them at 400 F for 8-10 minutes until crisp.

For assembling the chaat:
In a large serving bowl or plate, add one serving of shredded chicken, one serving of sweet potato. Sprinkle 1/2 a tsp of chaat masala on top of the chicken and sweet potato mixture.

Toss with a fork to mix. Sprinkle a little bit of the red onion, cilantro, and pomegranate arils on top. Now place the fried tortilla pieces on top and drizzle the cilantro chutney and tamarind chutney all over the chaat!

Reintroduction Notes: *You can add 1/4 tsp ground cumin (stage 1 reintroduction) to the chicken while cooking it.*

Recipe on next page

Mini Chicken Tostadas

Mexican food used to be one of my favorite foods in my pre-AIP days! Hence, creating this tostada dish made me very happy! You can use leftover cassava rotis for this recipe.

Serves: 2

Ingredients:

For the chicken:
1/2 lb. chicken thigh or breast pieces,
1/2 tsp turmeric
1 tsp dried oregano
1 tsp garlic powder
1/2 tsp sea salt
1 tbsp lemon / lime juice
1 tbsp olive oil or avocado oil
Avocado Oil for pan frying

For the refried beans:
1 cup canned pumpkin puree
1/4 tsp sea salt
1 tsp ground ginger

For the green sauce:
1 cup fresh cilantro
1 tbsp coconut milk
1 tbsp lemon juice
1 tbsp extra virgin olive oil
1/8 tsp sea salt

For the salsa:
1/2 of a small red onion finely chopped
1 tbsp lime/lemon juice
1/4 tsp sea salt
2 tbsp chopped fresh cilantro

For sour cream:
1/4 cup coconut cream
1 tsp lemon/lime juice
pinch sea salt

For assembling the tostadas:
Mini cassava tortillas
shredded lettuce
avocado slices
1/2 cup cilantro coconut chutney (per recipe on page 205)

Method:

For the crisp mini tortillas:
Follow the cassava roti recipe (on page 159) and make a dough. Divide dough into 12 balls and roll each ball to about 2 inches in diameter. (You can also use leftover rotis/ tortillas)

Heat about 1 cup avocado oil in a deep frying pan and deep fry the tortillas one at a time until they are crisp (about 2 mins). Remove using slotted spoon and place on paper towels.

Alternatively, you can first cook the tortilla on a pan. When cooked all the way through, apply oil on both sides and then place on a baking tray lined with parchment. Bake at 400 F for 10-12 minutes until crisp.

Cooking the Chicken:
Mix the chicken in all the marinade ingredients and keep aside for 10-15 minutes.

Heat a frying pan or skillet and add the oil. When hot add the chicken pieces and cook for 3-4 minutes and then flip to other side. Cook for a couple more minutes and transfer to a dish.

For the 'refried beans':
In a small sauce pan, add all the ingredients and cook for about 5 minutes till some of the water evaporates and you get a creamy thick consistency. Turn heat off and keep aside.

For the salsa:
Combine all ingredients in a small serving bowl. Keep aside.

For sour cream:
Combine all ingredients in a small bowl and whip to a smooth creamy consistency using a spoon.

For assembling the tostadas:
Serve tostadas by taking a fried (or baked) mini tortilla, adding a layer of the pumpkin mixture, then shredded chicken on top. Top with green chutney sauce, salsa, lettuce and avocado. Serve with sour cream on the side!

Reintroduction Notes:
You can add half a teaspoon of ground cumin (stage 1 reintroduction) while cooking the chicken and the beans.

Crispy Calamari

Calamari was always a favorite of our family while eating out. Now I make this AIP version for the whole family and we all love it! The toasted coconut chips, garlic and curry leaves give it an Indian twist!

Serves: 2-3 (paired with a salad)

Ingredients:

1 lb. of squid (mix of tubes and tentacles)
⅓ cup cassava flour
1/4 cup tapioca flour
1 tbsp garlic powder
1/2 tsp turmeric powder

Coconut Oil or Avocado Oil for frying

For garnish:
1 tbsp extra virgin coconut oil
1/2 cup coconut chips or frozen sliced coconut
4 large garlic cloves, peeled and thinly sliced
8-10 fresh curry leaves (optional)

Method:

Cut the squid tubes in 1/4 inch thick pieces. Cut each tentacle in half length-wise. Using paper towels, try to absorb the moisture from the squid as much as possible. Keep aside.

In a paper bag or a ziploc bag, add the flours, the garlic powder and turmeric powder. Close the bag and shake vigorously to mix everything well. Then drop the squid inside the bag and shake again for a few seconds to allow all the squid to be coated with the flour blend.

Heat a stainless steel skillet and when hot add the oil for shallow frying. Add enough oil to come up to about 1/4 inch of the pan and lower heat to medium.

When the oil is hot, drop each squid piece one by one into the oil carefully. Add just enough to fill the pan and have room for you to flip them easily.

Fry for about 2 minutes on one side and then carefully flip each squid piece using a fork or a spatula. Cook on the other side for about 1 more minute till the squid is crisp on both sides.

Transfer to a dish lined with paper towels to catch excess oil.
Finish frying all the rest of the squid this way.

For the garnish, wipe off the excess oil and flour from the skillet and add the coconut oil. When hot add the coconut chips or slices, the garlic and the curry leaves.

Saute for about 2 minutes on medium heat until they turn slightly brown and crisp. Turn heat off and add this mixture to the fried calamari and serve while hot!

Notes:
You can also deep fry the squid in a deep frying pan. The frying time may be a little less when you deep fry vs. shallow fry.

Chicken Liver Masala

My grandmother used to make the best chicken livers! This version is an adaptation of her original version. The key is lots of onions and herbs!

Serves: 3-4

Ingredients:

About 1 lb. (18 oz) organic chicken livers
2 tbsp extra virgin coconut oil
2 medium size red onions thinly sliced
2 bay leaves
2 tbsp finely chopped ginger
2 tbsp finely chopped garlic
8-10 fresh curry leaves, torn into pieces
1 tsp sea salt
1/2 tsp turmeric powder
1 tsp AIP garam masala (see recipe on page 222)
1 cup coconut pieces (fresh or frozen) or coconut chips
1 tbsp extra virgin coconut oil
1/2 cup fresh cilantro, chopped fine

Method:

Take the chicken livers from the freezer and thaw at room temperature for about 3 hours (or in the refrigerator for about 6-8 hours)

Reintroduction Notes: *You can add 2 tbsp coriander powder, 1 tsp black pepper powder and 1 tbsp fennel powder (all stage 1 reintroduction foods) along with the AIP garam masala to add an additional burst of flavor.*

In a large wide bottomed pan, add the coconut oil and heat. Add the onions and the bay leaves. Cook on low to medium heat for about 5 minutes until the onions turn soft and pink in color.

Now add the ginger, garlic and curry leaves. Stir fry for about 1 minute.

Next add the salt, the turmeric and stir. Cook for about 3-4 minutes.

Now add the chicken livers to the pan and cover and cook for about 5 minutes on low/medium heat. Open the lid and stir carefully to mix.

Then add the garam masala and the coconut pieces. Stir again to mix everything well (At this point, the livers would be partially cooked but still pink). Cover and cook again for about 5 to 7 minutes on low to medium heat.

Open the lid and check if the liver pieces are cooked (no bright pink color) and then using two large spatulas, try to break the large liver pieces into smaller pieces.

Add the 1 tbsp more coconut oil and the fresh cilantro and stir well to incorporate. Turn heat off.

Pan Fried Fish

In India, fish is mainly cooked in its whole form and with bones in! Mackerel and Sardines are great to pan fry whole! The recipe is very simple and can be used for any fish fillets as well.

Serves: 2-4

Ingredients:

Fresh or Frozen Whole Sardines, 4 medium size (or about 8 oz of any fish fillet)

For the marinade:
1 tsp turmeric powder
1 tsp ginger garlic paste* (recipe on page 220)
3/4 tsp sea salt
1 tbsp melted coconut oil or extra virgin olive oil

For pan frying:
About 1/4 cup coconut oil in batches
4 large garlic cloves, peeled and cut into thin long slices
6-8 fresh curry leaves

**optional*

Method:

If using whole sardines, clean the sardines by removing the scales and removing the internal organs. You can chop off the head or retain it if you like. Make shallow cuts all across the length of the fish to allow for the marinade to seep in. If using fillets, cut into half inch thick pieces. Dab dry the fish/fillet pieces with paper towels to remove excess water.

In a large mixing bowl, add all the marinade ingredients and mix well using a spoon. Now drop the fish into the bowl and using your hands, massage the marinade blend onto the fish making sure to get it into the cuts. Keep aside for 10-15 minutes.

Heat a stainless steel frying pan. When hot, lower heat to medium and add half the coconut oil. Add the garlic and the curry leaves and stir fry for 1 minute or so until the garlic turns golden and the curry leaves turn crisp. Using a slotted spoon, transfer the garlic and curry leaves onto a plate.

To the same pan, add the rest of the coconut oil and wait for a couple minutes until it is hot. Now drop the marinated fish one by one onto the pan. Let cook on medium for about 3 minutes. Then carefully flip them over and let cook for 2 more minutes on the other side.

Turn heat off and transfer the fried fish onto a serving platter. Top with the fried garlic and curry leaves and serve hot.

Reintroduction Notes:
You can add half a teaspoon of ground black pepper (stage 1 reintroduction) in the marinade.

SATISFYING

As the name implies, this section has recipes that are quite filling and sumptuous and thereby, a meal in themselves. Some of these like the Cod Lemon Rice, Fish Curry Chowder and Tuna Lettuce Wraps, I regularly have on rotation for my lunches! These do not take much time at all.

Chicken Biryani, Shrimp Tacos and Tandoori Chicken Pizza are super delicious and satiating and will surely make you feel extra special!

Fish Curry Chowder, Shrimp fried rice and Chicken Biryani are great for batch cooking for the week.

Shrimp, Mango And Sweet Potato Salad

This tropical salad is inspired by a Caribbean salad I once had. I substituted the regular potatoes with sweet potatoes and also added shrimp to make it a super delectable and satisfying meal!

Serves: 2

Ingredients:

12-14, medium size shrimp, thawed, peeled and deveined
1/4 tsp turmeric
1/8 tsp sea salt
1 tbsp coconut oil or avocado oil
About 1 cup, cucumber chopped into 1/2 inch slices (about 1 small cucumber)
2 celery stalks, chopped into 1/4 inch thick pieces
1 medium sweet potato (baked or boiled), peeled and cut into 1 inch cubes
1 medium ripe mango, peeled and cut into 1/2 inch cubes

1/2 cup cilantro coconut chutney (recipe on page 205)

Method:

Dab dry the shrimp with paper towels and place it in a bowl. Sprinkle the turmeric and salt on top. Keep aside for 5 minutes.

Heat a cast iron or stainless skillet and when hot add the coconut oil. Turn heat to medium and add the shrimp to the pan and cook for about 2 minutes on one side. Then flip and cook on the other side for 1 more minute. Turn heat off and transfer the cooked shrimp to a dish and keep aside.

To assemble the salad, toss all the vegetables and the mango into a large mixing bowl. Add the shrimp and then pour 1/2 of the green chutney and mix well. Serve salad warm or cold drizzling additional green chutney on top just before serving!

Fish Bhurji

This scrambled fish recipe is inspired by a Sri Lankan recipe. Bhurji is an Indian word for scrambled eggs and this bhurji, packed with flavor, makes up for the lack of eggs in AIP! This dish goes well with sautéed vegetables or a salad.

Serves: 2

Ingredients:

About 16 oz of flounder or any other white fish, thawed
1 tbsp coconut oil or extra virgin olive oil
1/2 of a medium red onion
1 tsp grated fresh ginger
4-5 fresh curry leaves (optional)
1/2 tsp turmeric
1/4 tsp sea salt
2 tbsp shredded coconut
1/4 cup finely chopped fresh cilantro leaves

Method:

Cut the fish into 1 inch by 1 inch pieces. Dry using paper towels. Keep aside.

Heat a stainless steel skillet and when hot add the oil. Then add the chopped red onion, ginger and curry leaves (if adding). Stir fry for 1 minute on medium heat. Then add the salt and the turmeric.

Now add the fish pieces and stir gently to coat the fish with the spices and the onion mixture. Turn heat to low and cover and cook for 2 minutes.

Open the lid and stir fry to scramble the now cooked fish into small pieces. Add the shredded coconut and the cilantro on top. Turn heat off.

Cod Lemon 'Rice'

Lemon rice is another staple southern Indian comfort dish where rice is flavored with lemon juice and other spices. This AIP version uses cauliflower rice and also includes fish to make it a satisfying and wholesome meal.

Serves : 2

Ingredients:

About 8 oz cod (or any other white fish) filets, cut into 2 inch by 1 inch pieces
1 tbsp extra virgin coconut oil
3 cups cauliflower rice (frozen or fresh homemade)
1 cup broccoli florets
1/2 tsp turmeric
1/8 tsp asafoetida
1 tsp grated fresh ginger
1/4 tsp sea salt
4-6 fresh curry leaves
2 tbsp fresh lemon juice

Method:

Take the fish filet and dab dry with paper towels to get rid off excess moisture. Keep aside.

In a medium size skillet, heat the coconut oil on medium heat. Add the cauliflower rice, broccoli florets, turmeric, ginger, salt and the curry leaves. Stir fry for about 30 seconds. Cover and cook on low heat for 5 minutes.

Open lid and place the fish filet pieces over the cauliflower rice and gently stir with a wooden spoon to mix the fish with the cauliflower rice (take care not to scramble the fish). Drizzle the lemon juice over the rice and the fish slowly.

Cover and again cook for about 2 more minutes until the fish is cooked all the way through. Turn the heat off. Transfer to a serving dish.

Chicken Biryani

Chicken Biryani can be called as the 'queen' of all rice dishes as it is a fragrant, delicately spiced and highly aromatic meal with layers of tender succulent chicken and rice interspersed with fried onions, fried nut and potatoes. This AIP version is equally delectable!

Serves: 2

Ingredients:

1/2 lb. chicken thighs (boneless) or breasts cut into 1 inch by 2 inch long pieces
1/2 tsp sea salt
1 tsp lemon juice
1/2 tsp ground turmeric
2 tbsp olive oil or avocado oil
1 bay leaf
3 whole cloves
2 inch long cinnamon stick
1 red onion thinly sliced
1/2 tsp sea salt
1 tbsp ginger garlic paste (recipe on page 220)
1 tbsp finely minced fresh mint leaves
1 tbsp finely minced fresh cilantro leaves
3 cups cauliflower rice fresh or frozen (if frozen, thaw to room temperature)
1/2 of a medium white sweet potato, peeled and cut into 1/2 inch by 2 inch pieces (like French fries)
2 tbsp water
1/4 tsp saffron threads
2 tbsp coconut milk

For garnish (optional):
golden brown crispy fried onions
golden raisins
fresh cilantro minced

Method:

Dab dry the chicken pieces with paper towels to get rid of excess moisture. Place them in a bowl and sprinkle the salt, turmeric and lemon juice. Mix using your hands to rub the seasoning onto the chicken pieces. Keep aside for 10-15 minutes.

Heat a large stainless steel skillet and add the oil. When hot, add the whole spices and let them toast for 30 seconds and then add the onions and the salt and cook on medium heat for about 8-10 minutes uncovered till the onions begin to turn brown and crispy.

Stir them every two minutes or so. Once the onions have browned, add the ginger garlic paste, the mint and the cilantro. Then add the marinated chicken pieces to the skillet and stir to mix the chicken with the onion mixture.

Next spread the cauliflower rice on top. Also add the sweet potato slices on top of the cauliflower rice. Sprinkle the water on top of the cauliflower rice. Lower heat to low and cover skillet with a tight fitting lid. Cook covered for 10 minutes.

Add the saffron threads and the coconut milk to a small bowl and microwave for 20 seconds. Stir to infuse the saffron into the coconut milk.

Open the lid on the skillet and splash the coconut milk and saffron mixture over the cauliflower rice. Check to see if the chicken is completely cooked and turn the heat off.

Serve the Biryani warm adding fresh cilantro, raisins and fried onions on top!

Reintroduction Notes:
You can add a handful of toasted chopped cashewnuts and almonds (both are stage 2 reintroductions) as a garnish.

Fish Curry Chowder

This one pot meal of fish and vegetables is absolutely delicious with the ginger and turmeric. The bacon just takes it over the top! This one is a must to try!

Serves: 2

Ingredients

2 tbsp coconut oil
1 slice of bacon, chopped
1 small red onion, chopped fine
1 celery stalk, chopped fine
3 cloves of garlic, chopped fine
1 tsp fresh ginger, grated
fresh curry leaves (or dried if fresh is not available)
1 cup, broccoli florets (fresh or frozen)
1 cup rutabaga cubed (or turnip or white sweet potato)
1/4 tsp sea salt
1/2 tsp turmeric powder
1/2 cup sliced mushrooms
1 cup chopped kale
About 8 oz, flounder filets, cut into large pieces
2 tbsp chopped cilantro or parsley
1/2 cup water
1 cup coconut milk
1 tbsp arrowroot starch plus 2 tsp tapioca starch mixed in 1/4 cup water

Method:

In a wide bottomed large cooking pot / sauce pan, heat the coconut oil. Add the chopped bacon and saute for 3-4 minutes on medium heat until the bacon gets toasted and crispy.

Next add the onions and the celery and saute for 2 minutes. Then add the garlic, ginger, curry leaves and saute for 30 seconds.

Then add the broccoli, rutabaga (or the sweet potato or turnip), the salt and the turmeric powder. Stir to coat the vegetables with the spices and cover and cook for 5 minutes on low to medium heat.

Open lid and add the mushrooms and kale. Stir fry for 2 minutes.

Then add the fish pieces, the fresh herb (cilantro or parsley) and stir very gently to mix (taking care not to break the fish into too small pieces) and add the water and cover and cook for 3-4 minutes.

Open lid and add the coconut milk. Check for seasoning and add more salt if needed.

Finally turn heat to low and add the arrowroot and tapioca starch slurry slowly stirring gently with a wooden spoon while adding until the soup thickens to a creamy consistency (about 1 minute). Turn heat off and serve soup warm.

Curried Shrimp Tacos

Tacos are another favorite meal of mine and they helped me to stay compliant on AIP as they are filling! Shrimp are easy to cook and so shrimp tacos are my favorite!

Serves 2-3

Ingredients:

To marinate shrimp:
About 15-18 large size shrimp, thawed, deveined and shelled
1/2 tsp sea salt
1/4 tsp turmeric
about 2 tbsp coconut oil for frying

For making tacos:
5-6 cassava tortillas (see recipe on page 159)

Other taco ingredients:
About 2 tbsp finely chopped red onion
About 1/2 cup finely shredded purple cabbage
1 ripe avocado, thinly sliced
1 tbsp finely chopped fresh cilantro
About 2 tbsp cilantro coconut chutney (see recipe on page 205)
About 2 tbsp sour cream (see recipe on page 226)

Method:

Place the shrimp in a medium size mixing bowl and dab with paper towels to remove excess water. Sprinkle the sea salt and the turmeric over it and using your hands mix all the shrimp with the seasoning mixture.
Keep aside for 10 –15 mins.

Frying the shrimp:
Heat a frying pan or skillet (stainless steel or cast iron) and add the coconut oil. Let it heat for about 2 mins and then add the marinated shrimp and pan fry for about 3 mins on medium heat.

Using a spatula or a fork gently flip each shrimp and fry on the other side for 1 more minute. Transfer to a plate. You may need to do this in batches depending upon the size of your pan.

Assembling the tacos:
Mix all ingredients listed under 'Other taco ingredients' except the green chutney and the sour cream, in a bowl.

Take each tortilla and place about 3 shrimp in the center. Smear some green chutney on both sides of the tortilla. Then add some of the onion cabbage mixture in the center. Spread a dollop of sour cream on top!

Assemble all tacos this way and serve!

Tuna Chaat Lettuce Wraps

'Chaat' stands for fast food that is tempting and usually has a mix of different flavors and textures! These lettuce wraps are super easy to make but pack a punch!

Serves: 1-2

Ingredients:

One 5 oz canned tuna
2 tsp AIP Chaat masala (recipe on page 224)
2 celery sticks, chopped
1/2 cup diced fresh cucumber
4-5 slices of pickled cucumber, chopped up
6-8 pitted green or kalamata olives, chopped or whole
3-4 pieces of organic canned artichoke hearts, diced
1 ripe avocado, peeled and sliced
6-8 fresh romaine lettuce leaves
fresh parsley or cilantro leaves, chopped
1 tbsp finely chopped red onion

For dressing:
1 tbsp extra virgin olive oil
1 tsp lemon juice
1/2 tsp AIP Chaat masala (recipe on page 224)

Method:

In a large mixing bowl, add the canned tuna (draining out water or oil from the can).

Sprinkle the chaat masala on top of the tuna and mix well using a fork.
Next add all the other ingredients to the bowl.

In a small mixing bowl, add all the dressing ingredients and stir to mix well. Pour this dressing on to the mixing bowl and stir to coat everything well.

To serve the wraps, place 3-4 lettuce leaves on a plate and scoop up some of the tuna mixture on to each of the leaves. Sprinkle the cilantro (or parsley) and the red onions on top and serve!

FARBERWARE

Recipe on next page

Tandoori Chicken Pizza

Everyone needs pizza in their lives whether they are AIP or not! This super delicious pizza utilizes an easy cassava flatbread and grilled chicken. The creamy turmeric 'cheese' sauce makes it 'over the top' delicious!

Serves 2

Ingredients:

For the pizza crust:
1 cup cassava flour
2 tbsp arrowroot flour
1/2 tsp sea salt
1 tsp nutritional yeast
1/4 cup coconut milk
2 tbsp extra virgin olive oil
About 3/4 cup hot water
extra olive oil for baking

For the topping:
Tandoori Chicken slices, about 1 cup (see recipe on page 112)
1 cup baby spinach leaves or mixed green leaves
1/2 of a small red onion, thinly sliced

For the 'cheesy sauce':
1/4 cup mashed cassava (or mashed white sweet potato)
4 frozen artichoke hearts (thawed and drained)
1 tbsp coconut milk
1 tsp apple cider vinegar
1/4 cup warm water
1/4 tsp sea salt
2 tbsp nutritional yeast
1/4 tsp turmeric

Method:

For the crust:
Preheat oven to 375 F.
In a mixing bowl, add the cassava flour, tapioca flour(or arrowroot flour), salt, nutritional yeast, the coconut milk and olive oil. Mix using spatula and then add the hot water slowly stirring carefully. Keep stirring using the spatula until all the water is absorbed by the flour. Now using your hands knead the dough until smooth.

Dough should feel very soft. Add the rest of the olive oil and this will make the dough extra soft and take any stickiness away.

Place the dough ball on a parchment lined large size baking tray. Flatten by pressing the dough slowly using your fingers. Form a 12 inch round crust this way. Prick the crust all over using a fork.

Slide the baking tray into the oven and bake for about 15 minutes. Get the tray out and brush the top of the crust with olive oil and slide it back into the oven for 5-7 more minutes until the bottom of the crust gets golden in color and slightly crispy. The crust should be still easily foldable like a flatbread.

Making the cheesy sauce:
Add all the ingredients listed under 'for the cheesy sauce' into a food processor and process until smooth and creamy. Keep aside.

To assemble the pizza:
Arrange the spinach (or mixed greens) leaves over the crust. Spread the tandoori chicken pieces on top. Using a piping bag or a ziploc bag, pipe the 'cheesy sauce' on top!

Note:
You can also use leftover curried chicken pieces from butter chicken (page 131) instead of tandoori chicken.

Shrimp and Vegetable Fried 'Rice'

Asian style fried rice is a family favorite in our home. I make it quite frequently as that is a great way to get my children to eat veggies! This AIP version is the best - even the 'rice' is a vegetable!

Serves 2

Ingredients:

1/2 cup of avocado oil plus 1 tbsp bacon fat
1 cup Broccoli florets
1 cup shredded cabbage
1 cup sliced mushrooms
1/2 cup carrots, cut into 1 inch and 1/4 inch thick pieces
About 1 tbsp more avocado oil if needed
1 tbsp ginger garlic paste (see recipe on page 220, or just use 1/2 tbsp. finely chopped ginger and 1/2 tbsp. finely chopped garlic)
12-14 large size shrimp, thawed, peeled and deveined
3 cups cauliflower rice (fresh or frozen)
1/2 tsp sea salt
2 tbsp coconut aminos
1 tbsp ume plum vinegar (or apple cider vinegar)
2 tbsp scallions, finely chopped

Method:

Heat a large bottomed pot or a pan / wok. Add the oil and the bacon fat. When the oil gets hot, turn heat to medium high and shallow fry each vegetable one at a time till crisp (for about 3 minutes each). Transfer to a plate.

When all the vegetables are cooked this way, there should still be some oil left in pan. If not, add about 1 tbsp more oil. Then add the ginger garlic paste and sauté for 30 seconds.

Then add the shrimp and stir fry for 1 minute and then add the cauliflower rice. Add the sea salt and stir to mix. Cover and cook for 5 minutes on low heat till the shrimp are cooked.

Open the lid and add all the fried vegetables back into the pot and add the coconut aminos, vinegar and the scallions. Stir to mix all the flavors into the vegetable and shrimp mixture. Turn heat off and serve warm!

Reintroduction Notes:
You can add 1/4 teaspoon of ground black pepper (stage 1 reintroduction) along with the other seasonings.

Anchovies with Coconut

Anchovies are an amazing nutritional powerhouse rich in omega 3 fatty acids as well as Vitamin B3 and Vitamin A. And they are delicious as is or as part of a dish! This is a traditional southern Indian recipe using whole anchovies (fresh frozen) and shredded coconut.

Serves: 1-2

Ingredients:

About 14-16 anchovies (fresh frozen; if using canned, see notes)
1/4 cup water
1/4 tsp turmeric
1 tsp fresh grated ginger
1/4 tsp sea salt
1 piece of kodampuli or tamarind (size of a nickel)
3 tbsp fresh frozen coconut (thawed) or dried shredded coconut
6-8 fresh curry leaves (you can sub fresh cilantro if you don't have curry leaves)
1 clove of garlic, peeled
1 tbsp coconut oil melted

Method:

In a small sauce pan, add the anchovies along with the water, salt, turmeric, ginger, and the kodampuli or tamarind. Place on heat and cook covered on medium heat for about 3-4 minutes until the anchovies are cooked.

Now take the lid off and let simmer for 2 more minutes on low heat until most of the water is evaporated. Turn heat off and keep aside.

In a small food processor, add the coconut, curry leaves (or cilantro) and the garlic and give it a couple pulses until the garlic and the herbs are all minced. (If using shredded coconut, add a tbsp of hot water)

Add this ground coarse paste to the anchovies and give a gentle mix. Transfer to a serving dish and drizzle the melted coconut oil on top. Serve with mashed yuca (recipe on p. 181) or steamed vegetables.

Notes:
If using canned anchovies which are already pre-cooked, reduce the water and cooking time by half. If you don't have tamarind or kodampuli, you can use some lemon/lime juice to impart the sourness.

COMFORTING

This section has recipes that are based on my comfort foods growing up. But I am sure that these will bring comfort to you as well!

Bone Broth is an essential component of healing and I highly recommend batch cooking this every week or every two weeks.

Daal or Lentil soup used to be my favorite comfort food so I missed it greatly when I first started AIP. This AIP version of Daal gives me the same comfort and I find myself licking the spoon!

Chicken Dumpling soup is another one that is very emotionally comforting to me reminding me of happy times from my childhood. This soup can be a meal by itself, and so can the cream of mussels and mushroom soup. All of the other soup recipes are light and need to be paired with something else like a protein and / a salad.

Bone Broth

Bone Broth is a perfect healing food that is so comforting as well. When I was a kid, my dad made Bone soup using goat bones whenever anyone fell sick in the family. This is that recipe except that I had to exclude whole black peppers to make it AIP.

Serves: 6-8

Ingredients:

2 lbs of grass fed beef bones or goat bones or carcass of a whole chicken
1 medium red onion or 2 small shallots, chopped
2 celery stalks, chopped
1 carrot, chopped
A 1 by 2 inch of fresh ginger root, peeled and chopped into thin rounds or big chunks
3-4 whole cloves
one 2 inch piece of cinnamon stick
1-2 bay leaves
8 cups water
1 tbsp apple cider vinegar
About 1 1/2 to 2 tsp sea salt

Reintroduction Notes:
You can add 4-6 whole black peppercorns (stage 1 reintroduction) along with the other whole spices.

Method:

Roasting the bones if using beef or goat bones (this step is optional):
Place the bones on a baking tray lined with parchment and bake at 400 F for 30 minutes. Remove from oven.

Using Slow Cooker:
Follow same procedure as for the Instant pot above and cook on slow heat for about 10 hours.

Now open the pot and remove the bones out and take out the bone marrow (if using beef or goat bones) and discard or save the bones (you can use them twice to make broth). You can add the bone marrow to the soup and drink the soup as is or keep the marrow separate and strain the rest of the soup through a large strainer or cheese cloth to get clear liquid.

Using the Instant Pot:
Add the roasted bones (if roasting) or the unroasted bones and everything else to the Insert pot and close the lid. Manually change pressure cook time to 2 hours. After the whistle goes off let it cool naturally until the valve goes down.

Beet Yogurt Soup

This light and subtly flavored beet soup is a great way to get beets into your diet. It is perfect for those meals when you want something light and you can pair with some protein or a small salad.

Serves 2

Ingredients:

1 tbsp coconut oil
1 cup grated beet (about 1 small)
1 tsp grated fresh ginger
5-6 fresh curry leaves
1/4 tsp sea salt
2 cups plain unsweetened coconut yogurt (see recipe on page 226)

Method:

Heat a sauce pan and add the coconut oil. When hot add the beet, the ginger, the curry leaves and the salt. Stir to mix and cover and cook on low heat for about 5 minutes or until the beets are completely cooked. Turn heat off.

Transfer the beet mixture to a blender. Add the coconut yogurt to the blender too and blend till you get a smooth creamy mixture.

Notes:
Instead of coconut yogurt, you can also use coconut milk with 1 tbsp lemon juice added to it.

Cauliflower Carrot Soup

This roasted vegetable soup with curry flavors is perfect for cold winter nights and also as breakfast. It is also easy to make. Double up the recipe and make a large batch.

Serves: 2-3

Ingredients:

1/2 of a large head of cauliflower, broken into florets
1 large carrot, scraped and diced into 1 inch pieces
1 medium size red onion, diced
1 tsp sea salt
1/2 tsp turmeric
2 tbsp avocado oil
4 large garlic cloves with skin on
1 medium size white sweet potato boiled and peeled
3 cups water or bone broth (to be used in divided portions)

Method:

Pre heat oven to 400 F. Line a large baking tray with parchment paper or aluminum foil.

In a large mixing bowl, add all the vegetables, sea salt, turmeric and the oil. Mix using your hands to coat all the veggies with the seasoning and the oil. Transfer the veggies onto the baking tray. Place the garlic cloves also on the tray.

Bake for about 30-35 minutes until all the veggies are cooked. Remove from the oven and cover with foil. Let cool for 5 -10 minutes.

After the veggies cool down, take the garlic cloves out carefully and press each of them gently to get roasted garlic puree out. Transfer that to a blender. Add all the vegetables to the blender too.

Roughly chop the boiled sweet potato into large chunks and add those to the blender too. Add half of the water (or the broth) and blend until all the vegetables are completely pureed. Open and stir to make sure there are no chunks. Then add the rest of the water(or broth) and blend again until creamy. Check for seasoning and add more salt if needed.

Serve soup warm or cold.

Shrimp and Vegetable Soup

This shrimp soup is not only delicious but also very restorative and healing owing to all the vegetables! The kombu gives it some extra umami but you can make it without it too.

Serves 2

Ingredients:

8-10 medium size shrimp, peeled and deveined leaving tails intact
1/2 cup ivy gourd, cut into long thin pieces (or use any other gourd or squash)
1/2 cup Daikon radish, cut into thin slices
2 medium taro root, peeled and cut into 1 inch cubes
1 cup bok choy, chopped
3 cups water
1 inch by 1 inch piece of fresh ginger root, peeled and cut into thick round slices
1/2 tsp organic turmeric powder
1/4 tsp sea salt
One 3 inch piece of kombu (dried seaweed) broken into 3-4 pieces

Method:

In a medium cooking pot, add the shrimp, the vegetables, ginger, turmeric and salt. Heat pot on stove and when the water starts to boil, turn heat to low and cover and cook for 6-7 minutes or until the taro pieces are well cooked.

Add the spinach/bok choy and cook for 1 more minute. Turn heat off.

Transfer to 2 serving bowls. Add the kombu (dried seaweed) pieces on top. Serve warm.

Chicken Dumpling Soup

This dumpling soup is an AIP version of a traditional southern Indian chicken dish that is made during Christmas. Although the recipe looks intimidating, it is really not that hard to do! Plus it is worth every effort!

Serves: 3-4

Ingredients:

For chicken curry:
1 lb. boneless chicken thigh pieces, cut into bite size pieces
1 large red onion, thinly sliced
1 by 1 inch piece of fresh ginger root, peeled and chopped fine or grated
6 garlic cloves, peeled and thinly sliced
8-10 fresh curry leaves (or dried curry leaves)
4 whole cloves (or you can use 1/2 tsp ground clove)
2 inch long piece of cinnamon stick (or use 1 tsp ground cinnamon)
1 tsp sea salt
1 tsp turmeric powder
1/4 cup finely chopped fresh cilantro leaves
2 tbsp melted extra virgin coconut oil
1/4 cup coconut chips (frozen or fresh)

For dumplings:
1/2 cup cassava flour
1/4 cup water chestnut flour (or tiger nut flour)
1/4 tsp sea salt
1 tbsp olive oil or melted coconut oil
1/4 cup mashed white sweet potato
About 3/4 cup hot water
1-2 tsp extra olive oil as needed

For making Soup:
3 cups water
1/4 tsp sea salt
1 clove garlic, thinly sliced
4-6 curry leaves
1/2 cup thick coconut milk

Method:

Chicken curry:
Add all the ingredients for the chicken curry to a wide bottomed cooking pot. Crush the onion slices using your hands to break them a bit and then close the lid. (It should be tight-fitting lid).

Slow cook for 10 minutes. Then open lid and stir and again close and cook on low heat for another 10 minutes. Turn heat off and keep aside. If using whole spices, discard them now.

For making the dumplings:
In a large mixing bowl, add the flours, the salt, oil and the sweet potato. Then slowly add the hot water while stirring the mix using a spatula.

Continue to add water until the mix looks completely wet enough to form a dough (you may not need the entire 3/4 cups of water). Let the mix cool for a couple minutes so that is cool enough to handle.

Then using your hands knead to form a smooth dough adding extra olive oil as necessary. Now divide the dough into about 12-14 equal balls. Keep aside.

Making the soup:

In a medium sized cooking pot, heat the 3 cups water along with the garlic and the curry leaves and the salt till the water starts to boil.

Now slowly add the dumplings to this and turn heat to low. Partially cover with a lid and let simmer for about 7 minutes until the dumplings are fully cooked. Now add the coconut milk and cook for 1 more minute and turn heat off.

For serving the soup , either you can mix all of the curry with the dumpling coconut milk mixture and serve individual portions out. Or for each individual serving, in a bowl, add some of the chicken curry followed by some of the dumpling mixture on top.

Creamy Mussels and Mushroom Soup

If you love mussels, you will love this creamy mussels and mushroom soup! I use pre cooked mussels for this recipe which makes it a cinch to make!

Serves 2

Ingredients:

1 tbsp coconut oil
1/2 of a medium size red onion, roughly chopped
4 garlic cloves, peeled and chopped
2 cups sliced mushrooms
1 tsp Italian seasoning (Make sure the brand you use is AIP compliant)
1/2 tsp dried thyme
1/4 tsp sea salt
1 tsp tamarind extract (or balsamic vinegar)
8 oz pack of frozen pre-cooked mussel meat
1 cup unsweetened canned organic coconut milk
1/2 cup water
1 tbsp arrowroot starch dissolved in 1/4 cup water

Method:

Heat a stainless steel skillet or a wide bottomed sauce pan. When hot add the coconut oil and then add the onion and garlic. Saute for 2 minutes and then add the sliced mushrooms.

Saute for 2 more minutes on medium heat stirring frequently. Then add the Italian seasoning, thyme, sea salt and the tamarinnd extract (or balsamic vinegar). Stir to mix and then add in the cooked mussel meat. Add the coconut milk and the water and let the mixture come to a boil.

Next mix the arrowroot starch with the water in a small bowl and add this slurry slowly into the mussel mixture stirring continuously with your other hand. Within a minute or so, the stew will thicken. Turn heat off and serve stew warm with some steamed veggies or over cauliflower rice.

Notes:
You can use fresh mussels instead of pre-cooked mussels just cook them in advance and deshell them before using in this recipe.

Reintroduction Notes: *You can add 1 tsp fennel powder (stage 1 reintroduction) along with the other spices to add an additional burst of flavor.*

Lentil Soup (Daal)

Daal, served with plain white rice, is one of the simplest and most comforting traditional Indian dish. I missed 'daal' a lot in my initial AIP days but never thought I could recreate that taste without lentils. And then one day I created this soup which tasted very similar to daal! Hooray!

Serves 4-6

Ingredients:

1 tbsp coconut oil
1 medium size red onion, chopped fine
2 celery stalks, chopped fine
1 tbsp garlic, chopped
1 tbsp fresh ginger, chopped
4-5 fresh curry leaves
1 tsp turmeric powder
1 tsp sea salt
1/2 cup fresh or frozen cranberries
2 cups pumpkin puree or spaghetti squash puree (homemade or canned)
2 cups water
1 cup full fat coconut milk (organic canned or fresh home made)
1/4 cup fresh cilantro leaves, chopped

Reintroduction Notes: *You can add 1 tsp ground cumin (which is a stage 1 reintroduction) along with the other spices.*

Method:

For Regular Pot:
Heat a wide bottomed large stock pot or a dutch oven. Add the coconut oil and then add the onions and celery. Stir and cook for 2 minutes on medium heat. Then add the garlic and ginger and curry leaves and stir on low heat for 1 minute.

Next add turmeric, salt and cranberries. Stir for 30 seconds. And add the pumpkin puree (or spaghetti squash puree) and water. Cover with a lid and cook on low heat for about 20 minutes.

Open the lid and add the coconut milk.
Using an immersion blender, puree the soup (or use a blender/food processor to blend)
Add fresh cilantro leaves and serve warm.

For Instant Pot:
Follow the same exact steps as above using sauté mode initially and then pressure cook for 10 minutes.

Manually release pressure and add the coconut milk. Using an immersion blender, puree the soup (or use a blender/food processor to blend)
Add fresh cilantro leaves and serve warm!

Cucumber Coconut Soup

Ash gourd or White pumpkin is traditionally used for this recipe. However, cucumber is a great option as well! This soup instantly transports me to Kerala! I learned this simple recipe from my mother in law as my husband is a big fan of this curry soup! Now my son enjoys it very much too!

Serves 4

Ingredients:

2 small cucumbers (seedless preferred), peeled and diced into 1 inch cubes
1/2 tsp sea salt
1/4 tsp ground ginger
1/2 cup water
2 cups full fat coconut milk (homemade or canned that is AIP compliant)
2 tbsp coconut oil
1/4 of a medium size red onion or 1 small shallot, chopped fine
6-8 fresh curry leaves, torn into pieces

Method:

In a medium sauce pan, add the cut cucumber pieces along with the salt, ground ginger, and the water, and place on the stove. Once the water begins to boil, cover and cook on low heat for about 5 minutes. Then take the lid off and simmer on low heat for another 5 minutes until almost all the water has evaporated.

Now add the coconut milk and continue cooking on low heat for another minute or so until the coconut milk begins to boil. Immediately turn the heat off. Keep aside.

Heat a small pan and add the coconut oil. Add the chopped onions (or shallot) and shallow fry until crisp and light brown. Turn heat off and add the fresh curry leaves. Pour this hot oil mixture on to the cucumber coconut milk mixture and mix. Serve soup warm.

Mixed Vegetable Sambaar Soup

Sambaar is another traditional lentil and vegetable stew cooked with a ground paste of toasted coconut and spices. Tamarind is used to impart sourness. My AIP version skips the lentils and cuts down the spices to achieve a similar rich and flavorful, nutrient dense soup.

Serves: 4

Ingredients:

2 medium size taro root, peeled and cut into 1 inch cubes
1/2 of a green plantain (strings removed and lightly peeled) cut into half lengthwise and then sliced into 1/4 inch thick pieces
1 medium size red onion, sliced
2 cups water
1 tsp sea salt
1/2 tsp turmeric powder
1 carrot, cut into 1/2 inch by 1/4 inch long pieces
1 zucchini, cut into 1 inch by 1 inch pieces
1 cup acorn squash, cut into 1/2 inch by 1 inch pieces
2 pieces of Kodampuli, washed (or 1 tbsp tamarind pulp or tamarind paste)
3/4 cup dried shredded coconut
1 clove of garlic, peeled and chopped
1 cup warm water, divided
1/2 tsp asafoetida
2 tbsp extra virgin coconut oil
4-6 fresh curry leaves

Method:

In a large stock pot, add the taro root, green plantain slices, onion, water, salt and turmeric.

Let cook covered on medium heat for about 7-8 minutes or until the vegetables are 75% cooked. Then add the rest of the vegetables and the Kodampuli (or the tamarind) and cook covered for 5 more minutes. Turn heat off and set aside.

Pre heat oven to 350 F. In a large baking tray lined with parchment paper, spread the dried coconut. Place the baking tray in the oven and bake for 5-7 minutes or until the coconut changes color to light brown. (Take care not to toast the coconut excessively)

Now add the chopped garlic to the tray and continue baking for 1 more minute and turn the oven off.

Transfer the coconut and the garlic mixture along with half the warm water into a food processor or blender and blend until you get a very fine consistency. Then add the rest of the warm water and blend again till smooth.

Place the pot with the cooked vegetables back on the stove and add the blended coconut mixture into it. Add the asafetida too and mix.

Cook uncovered on medium heat for 3-4 minutes more or so until the soup begins to boil. Turn heat off and check for seasoning and add more salt if needed.

In a small frying pan, heat the coconut oil and add the fresh curry leaves. Stir fry for 2 minutes until the curry leaves are toasted and add this oil mixture into the soup and mix well.

TANDOORI

Tandoori refers to food cooked in a tandoor which is a traditional clay oven with charcoal as the source of fuel that used to be common in rural India. For the purposes of this book, I have used the name loosely to include all recipes involving an oven. I use a convection oven however the temperatures mentioned in the recipe are that for a regular oven. But even so, I always recommend checking on doneness a couple of minutes before the recommended time as oven times vary greatly by the make of the oven.

There are four different chicken recipes in this section and each of them has a different flavor! Before AIP, I used to eat chicken only once or twice a week. On AIP, as I started eating it for multiple meals, I needed different flavors. With fish too, I used to usually only pan fry fish or make fish curry. But now I needed more options so that I didn't feel bored. And I also wanted the recipes to be quick and easy and what is what most of the recipes in this section are!

For the Hariyali Chicken, the Baked Fish with Mint Chutney and the BBQ Chicken recipes, having pre-made chutneys on hand will save you time!

Salmon Kebab

These salmon kebabs marinated with simple curry spices and lemon have so much flavor! These are great for an outdoor grill party!

Serves: 4-6

Ingredients:

4 wild caught salmon filets, about 4 oz each, cut into approx. 1.5 inch by 1.5 inch pieces
1 medium zucchini cut into 1 inch cubes
1 medium red onion, cut into 1 inch chunks

For the marinade:
2 tbsp freshly squeezed lemon juice
4 tbsp avocado oil
2 tsp AIP Curry powder (see recipe on page 221)
1/2 tsp sea salt
1 tsp dried parsley

Method:
In a large mixing bowl, mix all the marinade ingredients together and stir to mix well. Take 2 tbsp of this marinade and place in a smaller bowl for marinating the veggies.

Spread the salmon pieces on a tray or a cutting board and pat dry using paper towels. After getting rid off the excess moisture add them into the mixing bowl with the marinade and using your hands, gently coat each fish piece well with the marinade liquid. Leave aside for 5-10 minutes.

Add the veggies to the smaller bowl with the marinade. Keep aside.

You can grill the salmon using an outdoor grill , a grill pan or in the oven using broil setting. If you are using a grill pan, you do not need skewers. If using skewers, you can use metal skewers or wooden skewers. Pre-soak wooden skewers for about 1 hour in water.

Directions for Oven:
Pre-heat oven to Broil setting. Line a large baking tray with aluminum foil. Thread the marinated salmon pieces into the skewers alternating with the vegetables. Place tray on the uppermost rack about 6 inches away from the flame.

Broil for 4 minutes. Then remove tray and turn the skewers and let broil for 2 more minutes. Remove tray with the skewers and cover with aluminium foil to keep the kebabs warm and moist until serving.

Directions for grill pan:
Heat a grill pan and when hot, turn heat to medium and place the marinated salmon pieces and the veggies on it (may need to do in batches) and cook uncovered for 3 minutes. Then flip and cook for another 2 minutes. Transfer to a plate and keep covered until serving.

Cilantro Shrimp with Saffron Aioli

This grilled shrimp with a cilantro marinade is so easy to make if you already have pre-made cilantro chutney. The special saffron aioli makes the dish extra special without much effort!

Serves: 2-3

Ingredients:

16-18 medium size shrimp, peeled and deveined (you can leave tail on)
2 tbsp cilantro coconut chutney (see recipe on page 205)
1/4 tsp turmeric
1 tsp avocado oil

For the aioli:
2 tbsp coconut cream
8-10 strands of saffron
1/8 tsp of sea salt
1 tsp maple syrup
pinch turmeric

Method:

Blot dry the shrimp with paper towels.
In a large mixing bowl, add the cilantro coconut chutney, turmeric and the oil and stir to mix well. Then add all the shrimp to it and mix to coat the shrimp with the marinade mixture. Keep aside. Meanwhile, pre-heat the oven to broil.

Thread the shrimp on metal skewers (or pre-soaked wooden skewers) and place on a baking tray. Place the tray on the top rack about 6-8 inches from the broiler. Broil for about 5 minutes. Then turn the shrimp by rotating the skewers and broil for 1 more minute.

Take out from the oven and cover the shrimp with aluminum foil until serving.

For the Aioli:
Blend all the aioli ingredients in a small food processor until well blended and creamy. Transfer to a small serving bowl.

Serve the shrimp warm with the aioli.

***Reintroduction Notes:** You can add 1/2 tsp ground cumin (which is a stage 1 reintroduction) in the marinade for additional flavor.*

Tandoori Chicken

Tandoori Chicken is chicken marinated in yogurt, ginger, garlic and other spices and grilled in a special clay oven called as a Tandoor. This recipe tries to recreate some of the same flavors using a regular oven by using both the bake and broil settings.

Servings: 4

Ingredients:

1.5 lb. chicken thighs (boneless)
For the marinade:
2 tbsp ginger garlic paste (see recipe on page 220)
3/4 tsp sea salt
2 tbsp coconut yogurt (see recipe on page 226) or 2 tbsp lemon juice
1 tsp apple cider vinegar
1 tbsp AIP Garam Masala (see recipe on page 222)
1 tbsp avocado oil

Extra avocado oil for baking
lemon wedges and red onion slices for serving

Method:

Dab dry the chicken pieces using paper towels. Keep aside.
Add all the marinade ingredients into a large mixing bowl and mix well. Then drop the chicken thighs into the bowl.

Using your hands, coat the thighs well with the mixture. Keep aside for anywhere between 30 minutes to 8 hours or overnight. If keeping longer than 30 mins, place in the refrigerator.

Pre heat oven to 450 F. Line a baking tray with aluminum foil. Brush it lightly with Avocado oil. Then place the marinated thighs on the tray and bake at 450 F for 15 minutes. After 15 mins, take the tray out and flip the pieces and bake again for about 10 minutes more.

Take the tray out and change the oven setting to Broil.
Now place the tray back into the oven placing it on the top most rack about 6-8 inches away from the flame. Broil for 1-2 minutes or so until you see a couple char marks on the meat. Turn the oven off and take the tray out of the oven.

Cover the chicken with aluminum foil and keep covered until it's time to serve. Cut the thighs into 1/4 inch thick pieces and serve with a salad on the side.

Baked Flounder with Pudina (Mint) Chutney

This recipe is inspired by a western Indian fish recipe where the fish is coated with an herbed marinade and then steamed in banana leaves. In this recipe, I use a parchment paper parcel instead and the fish cooks beautifully!

Serves: 2

Ingredients:

Two 4 ounce flounder filets, thawed
2 tbsp of mint chutney (see recipe on page 211)
1 tbsp olive oil or avocado oil

Method:

Pre-heat oven to 350 F.

Line a baking tray with parchment paper.
Dab dry the filets using paper towels to absorb excess moisture and place them on one half of the baking tray.

Coat the filet on both sides with the chutney gently using your hands. Drizzle the olive oil over the filets.

Fold the parchment paper over the filets so as to cover them and form a loose package.

Place tray in the oven and bake for 15 minutes.
Take out of the oven and serve warm with cauliflower pilaf or a salad.

Hariyali (Green) Chicken

This 'green' chicken is inspired by a similar grilled chicken dish that our family used to enjoy at a local Indian restaurant. Even without the green chillies, this chicken has tons of flavor from the ginger, garlic and cilantro. And all that spinach in it just makes me extra happy!

Serves: 2-3

Ingredients:

About 1 pound chicken thighs (boneless)
2 cups fresh spinach leaves
2 cloves of garlic
2 inch by 1 inch piece of fresh ginger or 1 tbsp grated fresh ginger
1/4 cup of fresh cilantro leaves
3/4 tsp sea salt
1 tbsp freshly squeezed lemon juice
1 tbsp water
About 2 tbsp avocado oil or olive oil for baking

Method:

Cut the chicken thighs into smaller (about 2 inch by 2 inch) pieces. Dab dry using a paper towel. Keep aside.
Boil some water in a small sauce pan and when the water starts to boil, add the spinach leaves and let cook for about 2 minutes. While the spinach is cooking, take a medium size mixing bowl and fill about 1/2 of it with ice. As soon as the spinach cooks (at the 2 minute mark), turn the heat off and using a strainer drain the water from the spinach. Now quickly add the cooked spinach into the bowl with the ice. Using a pair of tongs place all of the spinach under the ice to cool it quickly.
Keep this bowl aside. In a small food processor jar, add all the rest of the ingredients.

Then carefully remove the cooled spinach leaves from the ice bowl and add them to the food processor. (Make sure to only get the spinach and not any ice or water as additional water will change the consistency of the marinade). Blend everything till you get a smooth consistency. Transfer to a large mixing bowl.

Preheat oven to 400 F.
Line a baking tray with aluminum foil or parchment paper and brush lightly with oil. Take about 2 tbsp of the marinade from the bowl and keep it aside for later.

To the rest of the marinade in the mixing bowl, add the chicken pieces and coat each piece with the marinade using your hands. Keep aside for 15 minutes.

Then place the chicken pieces on to the foil (or parchment paper) lined tray and place the tray in the oven.

Set timer for 15 minutes. After 15 mins, remove the tray brush the tops with oil and flip the pieces over and place tray back in the oven for 8-10 more minutes or until the chicken has some golden brown spots.

Do not over cook as the chicken will turn dry. Remove tray from the oven and cover with foil or parchment paper until serving.

Serve the chicken warm by placing the chicken pieces on a plate and drizzling the reserved green sauce on top.

Turmeric Lemon Chicken

This baked chicken is moist and oozing with flavor from the turmeric, lemon juice and the Italian seasoning! I recommend chicken thighs for this recipe!

Serves: 2

Ingredients:

About 1 lb. chicken thighs (boneless; you can also use chicken breasts)
1 tsp sea salt
1/2 tsp turmeric powder
1/2 tsp Italian seasoning
1/2 tsp garlic powder
1/2 tsp dried thyme
1 tbsp lemon juice
1 tbsp extra virgin olive oil
extra olive oil for the pan

Method:

Preheat oven to 400 F.
Line a baking tray with aluminum foil or parchment paper.

Once thawed, blot dry the chicken thighs with paper towels and place them side by side on the baking tray.

Sprinkle the salt, all the spices and the lemon juice and olive oil on top of the thighs.
Using your hands gently massage the spices on to the chicken pieces making sure they are evenly distributed.

Place the tray in the oven and bake at 400 F for 15 minutes first. Then flip the chicken pieces and bake again for 10-12 minutes until the bottoms have slight golden spots. (If using chicken breasts, bake for about 20 minutes total, 15 plus 5)

Take out from the oven and cover with aluminum foil until serving.

Note: Oven times are with respect to a convection oven and conventional ovens may take more time than that.

Barbecue Chicken

This Barbecue chicken is finger licking delicious! And the barbecue sauce (aka tamarind chutney) has only 3 ingredients!

Serves: 2

Ingredients:

1 lb. chicken thighs (boneless), about 4 pieces
1 tsp ground ginger
1/4 tsp sea salt
About 2-3 tbsp tamarind chutney, divided (see recipe on page 208)

Method:

Preheat oven to 400 F.
Line a baking tray with aluminum foil or parchment paper.

Once thawed, blot dry the chicken thighs with paper towels and place them in a mixing bowl. Add the salt, ground ginger and 1/2 tbsp of the tamarind chutney onto the chicken. Using your hands gently massage the marinade on to the chicken pieces.

Place the tray in the oven and bake at 400 F for 15 minutes first. Then flip the chicken pieces and bake again for 5 more minutes. Take out from the oven and cover with aluminum foil until serving.

Just before serving, cut the thighs into slices and place on a serving plate. Drizzle the extra tamarind chutney on top!

CURRIES AND STEWS

This section is highly inspired by the foods I grew up eating! Curries are the mainstay of Indian cuisine and initially on AIP, I was challenged since both rice and roti (whole wheat flatbread) were not allowed. Hence discovering cassava four and learning how to make rotis from that was a game changer for me! Seriously! Once I could eat my curry and roti, I felt that I could do this! I am sure many folks with similar ethnic backgrounds as myself will relate to this!

While listing recipes for this section, I had to eventually control myself and limit the list to a few since there were one too many! And yes each one of these I love! This includes beef, chicken, fish and pork curries. If I had to pick one, I would pick pork vindaloo as my most favorite one, which is adapted from my paternal grandmother's vindaloo recipe. The three fish recipes here are each different and unique in their own way and I will highly encourage you to try all of them! Eating fish in different ways is a good way to get yourself to eat more fish.

The Creamy Chicken and Vegetable Stew can be a meal in itself while all the other recipes in this section can be paired with a flatbread of some kind , a vegetable side or a salad.

Kerala Beef Stew

The curry base for this stew is a traditional southern Indian (Keralan) base. Fresh coconut is first grated, then toasted and then ground with many different spices to yield this beautiful curry sauce. Toasting coconut is usually done by stir frying it on a pan on the stove. That is a tiresome process and so I figured out an easier way using an oven.

Serves: 4-6

Ingredients:
2 lbs beef stew meat (grass fed), cut into 1 inch cubes
4 whole cloves
2, one inch cinnamon sticks
1 bay leaf
2 tbsp finely chopped fresh ginger
1/2 tsp turmeric
3/4 tsp sea salt
1/4 cup water
1 cup dried shredded coconut
2 tbsp coconut oil
2 red onions, thinly sliced
4 garlic cloves, finely chopped
6-8 fresh curry leaves
1 tsp ground cinnamon
3 taro root, peeled and chopped
2 cups water, divided

Method:
In a large cooking pot, add the meat along with the whole spices, ginger, turmeric and salt. Mix using your hands to let the spices get on top of all the meat pieces.

Reintroduction Notes: *You can add 2 tbsp coriander powder, 1 tsp black pepper powder, 1 tsp cumin powder and 1 tbsp fennel powder (all stage 1 reintroduction foods) along with the other spices for a more authentic curry flavor.*

Add the water. Cover with a tight fitting lid with no opening and cook on low heat for 15 minutes. Turn heat off. Keep aside. (You can also use an Instant Pot for this step and pressure cook for 7 minutes. Release pressure naturally).

You can at this point discard the whole spices if you like. While the meat is cooking, turn the oven to 350 F.

In a baking tray lined with parchment paper, spread the shredded coconut evenly. Place this tray inside the oven and bake for about 5-6 minutes until the coconut turns golden brown. Take out of the oven and keep aside.

Heat a large sauté pan or a wok style pan and when hot, add the coconut oil. Add the sliced onions and garlic and sauté for 2 minutes on medium heat. Then add the garlic, curry leaves and cinnamon and sauté for 1 more minute.

Turn heat off and transfer this onion mixture to a blender or a food processor. Add half of the water and also the toasted coconut. Blend carefully (opening blender lid frequently to release any steam) for 1-2 minutes until you get a fine paste.
Transfer this paste to the cooking pot with the beef.

Rinse the blender jar with the rest of the water and add this to the stew pot too. Add the chopped taro pieces.

Stir everything together and again cover and cook for 5-7 minutes on medium heat until the taro is fully cooked.

Creamy Chicken and Vegetable Stew

This creamy chicken stew is a one pot meal that is delicious, nourishing and so easy to make too! Whole spices like cinnamon and cloves as well as fresh ginger gives it loads of flavor!

Serves: 4-6

Ingredients:

2 tbsp avocado oil or olive oil
1/2 of a large red onion, chopped fine
2 celery stalks, diced
1/2 cup of sliced mushrooms
1 carrot, peeled and diced
1 white sweet potato, peeled and diced (you can use regular sweet potato too)
1 1/2 tsp sea salt
1 bay leaf
One 2 inch piece of cinnamon stick
3 whole cloves
1 inch by 1 inch piece of fresh ginger peeled and chopped fine
1 tsp dried thyme
1 1/2 lbs chicken breasts or skinless chicken thighs (boneless), cut into bite size pieces
3 cups water
1 cup coconut milk (I like to use Aroy D brand)
2 cups fresh kale leaves chopped
3 tbsp arrow root starch mixed with 1/4 cup water

Method:

Heat a large stock pot and add the oil. Let heat for 30 seconds and then add the onions, celery, and mushrooms. Saute for 1 minute and then add the carrot and the sweet potato. Add the salt, cinnamon sick, whole cloves, ginger and thyme. Stir to mix well with the veggies.

Then add the chicken pieces. Pour the water and let cook until the water comes to a boil. Then lower the heat and let cook covered for 15 minutes. Open the lid and add the coconut milk and the kale. Stir to mix and let cook uncovered for 5 more minutes.

Meanwhile, in a small bowl, mix the arrowroot starch with the water until it forms a smooth slurry.

Pour this slurry into the pot and stir slowly using a spoon for about 2-3 minutes until you can feel the sauce thicken.

Check soup for seasoning and add more salt if needed. Discard whole spices before serving.

Note: You can place all the whole spices – bay leaf, cloves and cinnamon in a muslin cloth bag like a bouquet garni and then place it in the pot to make it easier to discard before serving.

Fish Tikka Masala

In this Fish Tikka Masala, the fish is marinated first with ginger and garlic and lightly pan fried. Then it is further cooked in a delicious, creamy tikka sauce. Cod fish works great in this recipe however Salmon or any other fish with a thick filet will work too.

Serves: 4

Ingredients:

1 pound (16 oz) of salmon or cod filets (wild caught)
2 tbsp of ginger garlic paste (see recipe on page 220) in divided portions
1/4 tsp sea salt
2-4 tbsp coconut oil for pan frying
1 medium red onion
1⁄2 cup cranberries fresh or frozen (frozen should be thawed)
1⁄4 teaspoon ground turmeric
1⁄2 tsp sea salt or as needed
1/4 cup coconut milk
1 cup water
1 tablespoon freshly squeezed lemon juice (optional)
fresh cilantro and thinly sliced onions for garnish

Method:

Cut the fish filet into small pieces (about 2 inch by 1 inch thick each). On each piece, score small shallow cuts on top using a paring knife so the marinade can get in. Dab with paper towels to remove all water from the surface of the fish. Place the fish in a mixing bowl.

Take half of the ginger garlic paste and add it to the fish pieces and add the sea salt too. Mix well using your hands to coat the pieces well. Keep aside for 5-10 minutes to marinate.

Heat a frying pan/skillet and when hot, add about 2 tablespoons of the coconut oil and heat on medium heat for 30 seconds.

Add the marinated fish pieces skin side down (you may need to do in two batches) and cook for 3 minutes on one side. Then flip each piece carefully and cook for 2 more minutes. Transfer the fish filets to a dish.

Now to the same pan, add the onion and cranberries. Stir fry for 2 minutes. Add the rest of the ginger garlic paste too. Stir fry for 30 seconds and add the turmeric and salt.

Cover and cook for 3-4 minutes on low. Turn heat off and transfer this mixture along with the coconut milk and half of the water to a food processor or a blender and blend until you get a fine consistency sauce.

Pour this blended mixture back to the same pan. Rinse the food processor jar with the rest of the water and add that to the pan too.

Let the mixture come to a simmer (about 2 minutes) and turn heat to low. Add the lemon juice (if adding) and check for salt and add more salt if needed.

Finally, add the fried fish pieces into the sauce and let simmer for one minute. Turn heat off and garnish with thinly sliced red onions and fresh chopped cilantro. Serve with cauliflower rice or cassava rotis/tortillas.

Reintroduction Notes:

You can replace the cooking oil with grass-fed ghee or butter (Stage 1 Reintroduction)

'Butter' Chicken

Butter Chicken is a dish that has loads of butter (or ghee) and the gravy is made from lots of tomatoes and dairy to give you a velvety smooth curry. I tried to create an AIP version that is night shade free and dairy free but yet delicious!

Serves: 4

Ingredients:

1.5 lbs of chicken thighs (boneless), cut into 1x2 inch pieces
1 tsp ground ginger
1 tsp garlic powder
3/4 tsp sea salt
1 tbsp lime juice (or apple cider vinegar)
2 tbsp coconut oil or avocado oil
1 tsp kasoori methi (dried fenugreek leaves)
1 inch by 1 inch piece of Dagad phool / Stoneflower (optional)
one piece of whole mace (or 1/2 tsp ground mace)
2 medium size red onions chopped roughly
1/2 tsp sea salt
10-12 fresh or frozen cranberries
1/2 cup pumpkin puree (canned or homemade)
1 cup water
1/2 tsp ground cinnamon
1 tsp coconut sugar or honey or maple syrup (optional)

Method:

In a large mixing bowl, add the chicken pieces, the garlic powder, ground ginger, sea salt and the lime juice (or apple cider vinegar). Mix with your hands to coat the chicken well and keep this aside.

Place a large cooking pot and heat the oil. When hot, add the kasoori methi (dried fenugreek) and the dagad phool (if adding), the onions and the sea salt. Stir fry for a couple minutes.

Next add the marinated chicken and cranberries and stir fry for 3-4 minutes on medium heat. Then add the pumpkin puree, water, cinnamon and sweetener (if adding).

Cover and cook on low heat for 15 minutes or until the chicken is cooked and soft. Continue to simmer uncovered for a couple more minutes until you get the desired consistency for the curry. Serve Butter Chicken with grain free cassava rotis or with cauliflower rice.

Note: If you want a smooth gravy (sauce), then after the curry is done cooking, you can take the chicken pieces out and blend the curry sauce using a hand blender(or blender) and then add the chicken pieces back in.

Tangy Fish Curry

This fish curry is mine and my family's absolute favorite. It is a traditional recipe cooked in an earthen pot that uses 'kodampuli' for giving it a tangy and smoky flavor. You can also make this curry using shrimp instead of fish.

Serves: 3-4

Ingredients:

2 pieces of Kodampuli (or 1 ping pong ball size piece of tamarind paste)
1/2 cup hot water
About 1 lb. of bone-in mackerel fish or any thick fish filet, cut into about 1 inch by 2 inch pieces
1 inch by 1 inch piece of fresh ginger, finely chopped or grated
3/4 tsp turmeric powder
1 tsp sea salt
3/4 cup canned coconut milk (AIP compliant brand) or homemade coconut milk
For the garnish:
2 tbsp melted extra virgin coconut oil
2 tbsp finely chopped red onions or shallots
6-8 fresh curry leaves

Method:

Wash the kodampuli pieces to get rid off any sand or salt. Then soak them in the hot water for about 10-15 minutes until they get soft. (If using tamarind, soak the tamarind paste in hot water for 10-15 minutes and then strain the pulp through a fine mesh strainer to get the extract.) Keep the soaked kodampuli or tamarind extract aside.

In a large cooking pot (earthen would be excellent,) add the fish and all the rest of the ingredients. Stir using a spoon to blend the spices in the coconut milk mixture. Then add either the soaked kodampuli pieces along with the soaked water or the tamarind extract (if using tamarind) into the pot as well.

Place the pot on the stove and cook on medium heat uncovered for 5 minutes or until the mixture begins to boil. Then turn heat to a low simmer and cover the pot using a lid keeping it slightly ajar to let steam out. Cook this way for about 10 minutes until the fish is cooked. Turn heat off.

Heat a small frying pan and when hot add the coconut oil. When the oil gets hot, and the onions and the curry leaves. Stir fry for about 2-3 minutes until the onions turn golden brown and the curry leaves turn crisp.

Turn heat off and pour this oil mixture over the fish curry and stir to mix. Serve warm with mashed cassava or cassava rotis or cauliflower rice on the side.

Note:
You can also make this curry using shrimp instead of fish!

Pork Vindaloo

This is my paternal grandmother's recipe and this is my most favorite way to eat pork. Despite excluding the hot red chilli peppers, this sour and sweet AIP version is quite delectable. Make sure you get a cut of pork that has a lot of fat as that's what makes this curry so flavorful!

Serves: 4

Ingredients:

2 lbs (about 1 kg) pork chops (or pork belly), washed and cut into small 1 inch cubes (retain all the fat)
2 by 2 inch fresh ginger root, peeled
20 pearl onions or 1 medium size red onion, roughly chopped
10 garlic cloves, peeled
3/4 tsp turmeric
6-8 cranberries fresh or frozen
1 tsp sea salt
2 sprigs fresh curry leaves
2 tsp coconut oil
1 / 2 cup thinly sliced coconut chips (frozen or dried)
1 cup water
2 tsp apple cider vinegar
1 tsp coconut sugar
additional extra virgin coconut oil to drizzle on top

Method:

In a small food processor, blend the onion, ginger and garlic together to get a fine paste.

In a large cooking pot, add the pork , the above blended mixture and the sea salt. Add turmeric, cranberries and curry leaves and the coconut oil.

Then, add the coconut chips (pieces.) Add one cup water and mix everything well and cover and cook on low heat for 30 minutes.

Open the lid and add the apple cider vinegar and coconut sugar. Stir to mix. Turn heat off.

Check for salt and add more if needed. Drizzle extra coconut oil on top. Serve with cauliflower 'rice' or with cassava rotis.

Reintroduction Notes: *You can add 1/4 tsp mustard powder, 1/4 tsp black pepper, and 1/2 tsp fennel powder (all stage 1 reintroductiona) along with the rest of the spices.*

Shahi Chicken Kofta Curry

These melt-in-the-mouth chicken koftas in a rich and creamy curry flavored with saffron is sure to make you feel extra special! They taste great with a flatbread like rotis, naans or parathas.

Serves: 3-4

Ingredients:

For the Koftas:
About 1 pound ground chicken, thawed
1 tbsp ginger garlic paste (see recipe on page 220)
1/4 cup finely chopped fresh cilantro leaves
1/2 tsp sea salt
1/2 tsp turmeric
1 tbsp cassava flour
1 tbsp extra virgin olive oil or avocado oil

For the curry:
1 tbsp extra virgin olive oil or avocado oil
1 medium red onion, chopped
1 tbsp ginger garlic paste (see recipe on page 220)
1/2 tsp turmeric
1/2 tsp salt
8-10 fresh or frozen cranberries
1/2 cup plus 1 cup water
1/2 cup coconut milk
8-10 saffron strands
fresh cilantro leaves for garnish

Reintroduction Notes: *You can add 1/2 tsp ground cumin (which is a stage 1 reintroduction) along with the other spices to the kofta mixture.*

Method:

For making the koftas:
Add all the ingredients listed under 'Kofta' to a large mixing bowl and using your hands mix to uniformly mix the spices with the meat. Shape into small balls about 12 or so. Keep aside covered.

For making the curry:
Heat a large sauce pan or skillet and add the oil. When hot, turn heat to medium and add the onions and sauté for about 2-3 minutes until the onions turn soft.

Then add the ginger garlic paste and sauté for about 30 seconds. Now add the salt, turmeric, and the cranberries. Sauté for 1 more minute stirring and then add the 1/2 cup water and turn heat off.

Wait for a couple minutes to cool the mixture and then transfer to a blender and blend to a fine paste.

Now place the same pan back on heat and pour the blended mixture back into it.

Add the 1 cup water to it and let the mixture come to a boil. Add the coconut milk and the saffron strands. Now turn heat to low and slowly add the meatballs one by one into the pan.

Let it simmer uncovered for 5 minutes. Then flip each meatball carefully using a rubber or a silicone spatula and cook again for 5 more minutes until the balls are cooked through and the sauce thickens as well. Turn heat off.

Serve kofta curry with homemade grain free naan or with cauliflower rice!

Sri Lankan Chicken Curry

I am obsessed with 'chicken curries' and I love how a slight change in the spices or the ratio of the spices alters the taste of the curry! I am always looking for new recipes for chicken curries and this Sri Lankan version with a mix of Indian and Asian influences intrigued me enough for me to make an AIP version!

Serves: 4

Ingredients:

1.5 lbs chicken thigh or breast pieces cut into 2 inch by 2 inch pieces
1 large red onion thinly sliced
2 tbsp ginger garlic paste
2 tbsp coconut aminos
1/2 tsp sea salt
1/2 tsp ground cinnamon
1/4 tsp ground clove
1 tbsp tamarind paste/pulp (or 1-2 tsp tamarind extract)*
1/2 cup coconut milk
4-6 fresh curry leaves

** If using tamarind paste/pulp, soak in 1/2 cup hot water and extract the pulp.*

Method:

Regular cooking pot Method:
Place all ingredients in a large cooking pot and mix well using a spoon. Place a tight fitting lid on top and completely seal any valves or openings on the lid by placing a kitchen towel on top.

Cook on low heat for about 20 minutes. Open lid and check to see if the chicken is cooked through. Turn heat off.

Instant pot method:
Place all ingredients in the insert pot of the instant pot and mix well using a spoon. Close the lid and turn valve to sealing position.

Pressure cook for 5 minutes . Release pressure manually and open the lid.

Press sauté and cook on medium sauté for 2-4 minutes until the gravy thickens a bit. Press cancel and turn the instant Pot off.

Chicken Saag Curry

Saag is any curry with greens and adding in chicken makes the curry even more delicious! When my kids were younger, this was one of the ways I would sneak in leafy vegetables into their diet!

Serves: 4

Ingredients:

1 lb. chicken thighs (boneless) cut into bite size pieces (about 1 inch by 2 inch)
1 tbsp ginger garlic paste (see recipe on page 220)
1/2 tsp sea salt
1/4 tsp turmeric
6 oz or about 3 packed cups fresh spinach or a combination of spinach and kale leaves
2 tbsps coconut oil or avocado oil
1 bay leaf
2 cloves, whole
1 piece of cinnamon stick (about 2 inches long)
1/2 of a medium red onion, chopped
1 tsp ginger garlic paste
About 1/4 tsp sea salt
1 cup water
About 3-4 tbsps more coconut oil or avocado oil for pan frying

Method:

Blot dry the chicken pieces using paper towels. Then place it in a mixing bowl. Sprinkle with sea salt and add the ginger garlic paste and the turmeric.

Using your hands coat the chicken with all the spices and keep aside for 5-10 minutes.

Fill about 1/2 of a medium size sauce pan with water and place on heat for boiling. Once the water starts boiling, add the spinach leaves and lower heat to medium and let it cook for two minutes. While the greens are cooking, keep a large mixing bowl filled with about 2 cups of ice cubes ready.

As soon as the greens are cooked for 2 minutes, turn the heat off and then using a slotted spoon, transfer only the greens into the ice bowl. Let the leaves cool for a couple minutes and then discard all the ice from the bowl.

In the meantime, heat a skillet with the oil. Add the bay leaf , the cloves and the cinnamon stick. Then add the chopped onions and stir fry on medium heat for a couple minutes till the onions are softened.

Next add the ginger garlic paste and sauté for 30 seconds. Turn the heat off and transfer the entire mixture into a food processor jar or a blender, discarding the whole spices (bay leaf, cloves and cinnamon).

Add the cooled spinach leaves into the blender too and blend into a fine puree. Keep aside.

Now heat the same skillet adding a couple tablespoons of the oil. Heat on medium heat and when the oil is hot, add half of the marinated chicken pieces to the pan and let cook for about 3 minutes on medium heat.

Then flip them and cook on the other side for another couple minutes. Transfer to a plate. Repeat the same process until all the chicken is cooked. (we are only partially cooking the chicken at this stage).

Finally add all the chicken back into the skillet and add the blended green puree as well. Add the water to the food processor and blend once again to get all the puree out and add this to the pan too. Heat the skillet again on low for about 5 minutes to let the sauce thicken and to let the chicken cook completely. Turn heat off. Serve Saag Chicken with cauliflower rice or cauli pilaf or with homemade rotis!

Fish Molee

This is another traditional southern Indian fish recipe. It is tangy and sweet. The coconut milk balances all the spices. Any white fish will work well in this recipe.

Serves: 2

Ingredients:

2 tbsp extra virgin coconut oil or extra virgin olive oil
One 1 inch cinnamon stick
2 whole cloves
1 large red onion, cut into thin long slices
1 tbsp finely chopped fresh ginger
4-6 fresh curry leaves
1/2 tsp sea salt
1/4 tsp turmeric
4-6 fresh or frozen cranberries
2 small taro root, peeled and cubed (optional)
8 oz flounder or any other white fish filets, cut into 2 inch by 1 inch pieces
1 cup water
1/2 cup coconut milk
1 tsp apple cider vinegar

Method:

Heat a large wide bottomed sauce pan. Lower the heat to medium and add the oil. Then add the whole spices, onions, the ginger and curry leaves. Stir fry on medium heat for about 2 minutes. Then add the salt and turmeric and again stir fry for another 2 minutes.

Next add the cranberries and the taro pieces (if adding). Cover with a tight fitting lid and cook on low heat for 5 minutes or until the taro root pieces are cooked.

Next add the fish filets and the water. Gently stir using a wooden or silicone spatula to mix everything well and to ensure the fish filets are under the water level. Cover and cook for 2 minutes.

Open the lid and add the coconut milk, and continue to simmer on low heat for another 2 minutes.

Add the vinegar to the stew and stir it carefully so as not to break the fish apart.
Serve fish stew with cauliflower rice or cassava rice!

"CURRYTO" BOWLS

These bowls were mostly created by me as I tried to mix and match leftovers for my lunches! Since I work from home, I usually have a couple hours blocked during lunch. And many days I will be recipe testing and photographing during that time. One day I happened to make the turkey bowl where I made the turmeric mayo to go with it. I loved how the sauce made everything come together and so I started creating sauces (or chutneys) to match the contents of the bowls. In this section, I chose five different bowls with different flavors and I think they clearly demonstrate that AIP can be exciting! Just give your creativity a chance!

To create these bowls for lunch, you would need to batch cook or have the proteins cooked and ready in advance. The sauces are easy to make but you could have them ready in advance too. The Salmon Poke Bowl is one of our family's favorite dinners and it really comes together pretty easily!

Tandoori Shrimp and Kale Bowl

This bowl comes together pretty quickly even though the recipe may seem long. The cauliflower coconut rice is a nice touch and the raita sauce is a perfect complement to the shrimp!

Serves: 1-2

Ingredients:

For cooking the shrimp:
8-10 medium size uncooked shrimp (or 6-8 large), peeled and deveined
1/8 tsp sea salt
1/4 tsp turmeric
1 tsp ginger garlic paste (see recipe on page 220)
2 tbsp coconut oil or avocado oil
1 cup chopped kale leaves

For the cauliflower coconut rice:
1 tbsp coconut oil
1 bay leaf
1 cinnamon stick (1 inch long)
1 1/2 cups cauliflower rice (frozen or fresh)
pinch salt
1/4 cup water
1 tbsp shredded coconut

For the raita sauce:
2 tbsp coconut cream (top solid part from a coconut milk or coconut cream can)
1/2 of a small cucumber peeled and diced
1/4 of a small red onion or shallot, chopped
pinch kala namak (black salt) or sea salt

Other Optional Veggies/toppings for the bowl:
Boiled / roasted beets, chopped
Thinly sliced red onions

Method:
After thawing the shrimp, dab it with paper towels to remove all excess moisture and place in a mixing bowl. Add the turmeric, salt and the ginger garlic paste and mix with your hands to coat uniformly. Let sit for 5-10 minutes. Meanwhile heat a stainless steel or cast iron skillet and add the coconut oil. When hot, add the shrimp to it and cook on medium heat for about 2 minutes. Flip and cook again for 1 more minute. Then add the kale leaves and sauté together with the shrimp for 1 minute. Transfer to everything to a dish. Keep covered.

For making the cauliflower 'coconut' rice:
Heat a sauce pan and add the coconut oil. When the oil gets hot, add the bay leaf and the cinnamon stick. Then add the cauliflower rice and salt. Add the water and cover and cook for about 5-7 minutes or until all the water is evaporated and the caulirice is soft. Add the shredded coconut and mix. Keep aside.

For making the raita sauce:
Blend all ingredients for the sauce in a food processor until you get a creamy sauce. If the sauce is too watery, add some more coconut cream and blend again.

To assemble the bowl, take a large size bowl and place the 'caulirice' in the bowl. Then place the shrimp and Kale over it. Place the other veggies (if adding) in the bowl too. Drizzle the raita sauce over the shrimp and the 'rice'.

Salmon Poke Bowl with Teriyaki Sauce

Poke Bowls are a family favorite and they lend well to cooking for the whole family since I only need to cook additional white rice for the rest of the family. Teriyaki Salmon bowl is everyone's favorite and I love the AIP 'sticky rice'!

Serves: 4

Ingredients:
3 (4 oz) packs of wild caught salmon filets
1/8 tsp sea salt
2 tbsp olive oil

For the Teriyaki sauce:
1/2 cup coconut aminos
1 cup water
1 tbsp freshly grated ginger
1 tbsp chopped fresh garlic
1 tbsp finely chopped scallions
1 tsp raw honey
2 tsp arrowroot starch mixed with 1/4 cup water

For the sticky 'rice':
1 tbsp coconut oil
4 cups cauliflower rice (fresh or frozen)
1 cup coconut milk
1/4 tsp sea salt

For assembling the bowl:
About 3 cups, Steamed broccoli florets
1 Nori sheet, cut into ribbons
1 ripe avocado, sliced thinly
1/4 cup scallions, finely chopped

Method:
For baking the salmon:
Pre-heat the oven to 400 F. Line a baking tray with parchment paper. Place the Salmon filets on the tray and sprinkle with sea salt and olive oil.
Cover the tray with another sheet of parchment paper and place in the preheated oven for 15 minutes. Then take it out of the oven and keep covered.

For the teriyaki sauce:
Add all the ingredients listed under 'teriyaki sauce' except the 'arrowroot mixed in water' to a sauce pan and cook for about 5 minutes. Then take a small bowl and mix the arrowroot with the water to form a slurry and add this slurry slowly to the sauce pan stirring continuously using your other hand. Let continue to simmer on low until the sauce thickens up a bit. Turn heat off.

For the 'sticky rice':
Heat a sauce pan with the coconut oil. Add the cauliflower rice, the coconut milk and the salt. Cover and cook on low for about 7-8 minutes until the 'rice' is soft.

To assemble the bowls:
Divide the sticky 'rice' in 4 and place in 4 serving bowls.
Take the baked Salmon filets and cut them in large chunks using a knife. Divide these equally in the 4 bowls. Next divide the steamed broccoli, avocado slices the nori sheets and the scallions equally and place in all 4 bowls.
Finally drizzle the teriyaki sauce over all the bowls. Transfer the extra sauce in a separate serving bowl.

Ground Turkey Bowl with Turmeric Mayo

This bowl is also easy to put together once you have the ground meat thawed. A quick stir fry and an easy turmeric mayo makes it nourishing and satisfying!

Serves: 4

Ingredients:

For the meat:
1 tbsp coconut oil
1 lb. ground turkey (or ground chicken)
1 tbsp finely chopped garlic
1 tbsp finely chopped or grated fresh ginger
1/2 tsp turmeric
1/4 tsp sea salt
1/2 cup sliced mushrooms (optional)
About 2 tbsp fresh cilantro chopped

For the turmeric mayo:
1/4 of a ripe avocado
1 tbsp coconut milk
1 tbsp lemon juice
1 small clove of garlic
1/4 tsp turmeric
1/8 tsp sea salt
2 tbsp water

For assembling the bowls:
About 2 cups of steamed Broccoli and or other veggies (about 1/2 a cup for each bowl)
About 2 cups of Boiled or roasted sweet potatoes (about 1/2 a cup for each bowl)
1 ripe Avocado sliced (about 1/4 for each bowl)

Method:

Cooking the meat:
Heat a stainless steel or a cast iron skillet. Add the coconut oil. When the oil is hot, turn heat to medium and add the ground meat, garlic, ginger, turmeric and salt.

Stir well to mix and as the meat cooks, try to break the bigger chunks into smaller pieces. After about 5 mins, add the mushroom slices (if adding) and continue to stir fry for another couple minutes until both the ground meat and the mushrooms are well-cooked.

Cook on low for a couple more minutes until all the juices evaporate. Add the cilantro and mix. Keep this aside.

For the turmeric mayo:
Add all the ingredients listed under 'Turmeric mayo' and blend in a small food processor jar until smooth. If it feels too thick, you can add some more water. Transfer the mayo to a small bowl or a small jar.

Assembling the bowl:
In a serving bowl, add about 1/4 of the prepared chicken, the steamed veggies, the sweet potato and avocado slices. Drizzle the mayo on top!

Kerala Beef Bowl

This is a traditional Keralan meal and is popular in small street food shops all over Kerala. The Beef curry is spicy and it goes very well with the smooth and creamy yuca mash! In my AIP version, I use ground beef and I add spinach too!

Serves: 3

Ingredients:

For the Beef curry:
2 tbsp coconut oil
1 bay leaf
One 1 inch cinnamon stick
2 whole cloves
1 small red onion finely chopped
1 tbsp ginger garlic paste (or use 1/2 tbsp chopped garlic and 1/2 tbsp chopped ginger)
1 tsp AIP Garam Masala (recipe on page 222)
1/2 tsp sea salt
1/4 cup water
1 lb. grass fed ground beef
4-5 fresh curry leaves (use dried curry leaves if you cannot find fresh)
1 cup chopped fresh spinach leaves

For assembling the bowl:
3 cups creamy mashed cassava (see recipe on page 185)
finely chopped red onions
fresh cilantro, chopped (optional)

Method:

In a large cooking pot, heat the coconut oil on medium heat. When hot, turn heat to low and add the bay leaf, cloves and cinnamon. Then add the onions and stir fry for 2 minutes.

Next, add the ginger garlic paste, the garam masala and salt and stir fry for 30 seconds. Now add the water and stir. Then add the beef using a large spoon to break the lumps. Add the curry leaves too. Cover and cook for 10 minutes on low heat.

Open and stir making sure to break any big chunks of the meat. Add the spinach and let simmer uncovered for 5 minutes until very little water is left. Check for seasoning and add salt if needed. Turn heat off.

To make the bowls:
Take a large serving bowl and add a cup of the mashed yucca mixture. Spread it to cover 3/4 of the bowl.

Then take 1/3 of the beef curry and pour into the bowl on top of the yucca. Sprinkle the red onions and cilantro (if adding) on top!

Chicken Kofta Bowl with Green Sauce

This is such a delicious and satisfying bowl! The soft and delicately flavored chicken koftas along with the curry sauce and the cilantro sauce will leave you asking for more!

Serves: 4

Ingredients:

1 recipe of Shahi Chicken Kofta Curry (see recipe on page 136)

For the cauliflower rice:
1 tbsp coconut oil
3 cups cauliflower rice (frozen or fresh)
1/4 tsp salt
1/4 cup water

For the green sauce:
1 ripe avocado
1/2 cup fresh cilantro
1 tbsp lemon juice
1/8 tsp sea salt
2 tbsp water
2 tbsp olive oil

cucumber sliced – about 12-16
fresh baby spinach leaves – about 2 cups

Method:

Prepare the kofta curry per the recipe on page 136.

To make the cauliflower rice:
Heat a sauce pan and add the coconut oil. When the oil gets hot, add the cauliflower rice and salt. Add the water and cover and cook for about 5-7 minutes or until all the water is evaporated and the 'rice' is soft. Turn heat off and keep aside.

To make the green sauce:
Add all ingredients to a food processor and blend till you get a fine consistency. Keep aside.

For serving the kofta bowls, take a large serving bowl and add about 3/4 cup of the cauliflower rice. Spread it to cover half of the bowl. Then place 3 chicken koftas along with some curry on the top of the rice.

Place 3-4 cucumber slices and a handful of the spinach leaves on the other half of the bowl. Drizzle some green sauce on top of the cucumber and spinach.

BREADS

As I said before, being able to make cassava flatbreads was a game changer for me. And I am sure it will be for most folks that are newly starting on AIP, especially if they have had a history of eating breads and or rice.

It is fantastic to have an option for bread and so I have included different kinds of flatbreads I make regularly. The 'Satisfying' section includes a flatbread pizza, which I thought belonged in that section since it is a complete and satisfying meal by itself.

All the breads here can be paired with any curry or stew or also paired with any protein recipe from the 'Tandoor' or 'Tempting' sections. The 'Breakfasts' section also includes a couple flatbreads and I placed them there since those are traditionally eaten for breakfast in India.

One word of caution - These flatbreads can be tempting. To ensure that you continue to eat nutrient dense meals, indulge in them only occasionally. And when you do make them, they should only form a small part of your meal, with vegetables and proteins making up the most of your meal.

Cassava Rotis (Tortillas)

Once I discovered cassava flour and tried making rotis, my whole world of AIP changed for the better! Now, I could have my curries after all! Plus I could make great tacos using these!

Serves 3-4

Ingredients:

1 cup cassava flour
1/4 tsp sea salt
1 tsp extra virgin olive oil
1 cup hot water (that has been boiling)*
1-2 tbsp more extra virgin olive oil (as needed)
extra cassava flour for dusting

**Note: Different brands of cassava flour and sometimes even the same brand (at different times) can have different consistencies so the water quantity mentioned above is approximate. If the dough gets too wet, add a bit more flour. If you feel the dough is too dry, you can add a bit more hot water.*

Method:

In a large mixing bowl, add the cassava flour, salt and the oil.

Place a kettle filled with water on the stove to heat. Let it come to boil and then turn heat off.
Immediately measure the hot water and pour it into the bowl carefully. Use a spatula to mix the hot water into the flour mixture.

After a few seconds of mixing, test how hot the mixture is by slowly placing a finger into the bowl.

Once the mixture is cool enough to be handled (should be still warm), use your hands to knead the dough and make a smooth dough.

Add the additional 1-2 tbsp of olive oil as needed to make the dough smooth (should not be sticky). Divide the dough into small balls. (about 10)

Flatten each dough ball and then using a rolling pin flatten this ball to make a round (about 4 inches diameter).

Heat a cast iron (or non stick) skillet or pan and when hot turn heat to medium.
Place the rolled roti onto the hot pan. Let cook for 1 minute and flip to the other side. Now press the roti with a flat spatula and as you press it, it will start puffing up from all sides. Let cook for 1 more minute and then transfer to a tray.

Repeat the process for making more rotis as needed.
Leftover Rotis can be refrigerated for up to 4-5 days.

Note:
Wrap leftover rotis (tortillas) in aluminum foil and place in the refrigerator. To thaw, place them on a plate covered with a wet paper towel and microwave for 10 seconds.

Chapati

This Chapati is slightly different in taste and texture from the cassava rotis and they are quite similar to the traditional Indian whole wheat chapati. It is just soft, pliable and dense enough to sop up the curries.

Serves 3-4

Ingredients:

2/3 cup cassava flour
1/3 cup water chestnut flour (singada flour)
1/4 tsp sea salt
1 tsp extra virgin olive oil
1 cup hot water (that has been boiling)*
1-2 tbsp more extra virgin olive oil (as needed)
extra cassava flour for dusting

**Note: Different brands of cassava flour and sometimes even the same brand (at different times) can have different consistencies so the water quantity mentioned above is approximate. If the dough gets too wet, add a bit more flour. If you feel the dough is too dry, you can add a bit more hot water.*

Method:

In a large mixing bowl, add the cassava flour, water chest nut flour, salt and the oil.
Place a kettle filled with water on the stove to heat. Let it come to boil and then turn heat off.
Immediately measure the hot water and pour it into the bowl carefully. Use a spatula to mix the hot water into the flour mixture.

After a few seconds of mixing, test how hot the mixture is by slowly placing a finger into the bowl.

Once the mixture is cool enough to be handled (should be still warm), use your hands to knead the dough and make a smooth dough.

Add the additional 1-2 tbsp of olive oil as needed to make the dough smooth (should not be sticky). Divide the dough into small balls (about 10)

Flatten each dough ball and then using a rolling pin flatten this ball to make a round (about 4 inch diameter).

Heat a cast iron (or non stick) skillet or pan and when hot turn heat to medium.

Place the rolled chapati onto the hot pan. Let cook for 1 minute and flip to the other side.

Now press the chapati with a flat spatula and as you press it, it will start puffing up from all sides. Let cook for 1 more minute and then transfer to a tray.

Repeat the process for making more chapatis as needed.
Leftover Chapatis can be refrigerated for up to 4-5 days.

Note:
Wrap leftover chapatis in aluminum foil and place in the refrigerator. To thaw, place them on a plate covered with a wet paper towel and microwave for 10 seconds.

Pooris

Traditionally, Pooris were a treat for special occasions like religious festivals or weddings since they were deep fried. That proves the wisdom of our ancestors! You can make Rotis or flatbreads (to cook on a pan) from this same recipe for a 'healthier' bread.

Serves: 2-3

Ingredients:

1 cup cassava flour
2 tbsp water chestnut flour (singada atta) or 2 tbsp tiger nut flour
1/4 tsp sea salt
about 1 cup hot water
1-2 tsp extra virgin olive oil (as needed)
About 1 cup coconut oil or palm shortening for deep frying

Method:

In a large mixing bowl, add the cassava flour, water chestnut flour (or tigernut flour), salt and the oil.
Place a kettle filled with water on the stove to heat. Let it come to boil and then turn heat off.

Immediately measure the hot water and pour it into the bowl carefully. Use a spatula to mix the hot water into the flour mixture.

After a few seconds of mixing, test how hot the mixture is by slowly placing a finger into the bowl. Once the mixture is cool enough to be handled (should be still warm), use your hands to knead the dough and make a smooth dough.

Add the additional 1-2 tbsp of olive oil as needed to make the dough smooth (should not be too sticky). Divide the dough into small balls (about 20).

Heat a small wok or a deep frying pan/pot with the oil in it.

Flatten each dough ball and then using a rolling pin flatten this ball to make a round (about 2 inch diameter). Lay the pooris on a parchment paper.

Once the oil is hot, turn heat to medium high and fry each poori one by one. Fry till the poori puffs up and then flip on the other side and fry for 30 seconds more. Use a slotted spoon to drain excess oil and transfer to a plate lined with paper towels.

Repeat this frying process for all the rest of the pooris.

Naan without Yeast

Naan must be the most popular of all Indian breads in the whole world! So it needs no introduction. My goal was to make a version that was both AIP and yeast free. And I am proud of this recipe as this naan is soft and delicious!

Serves: 3-4

Ingredients:

3/4 cup cassava flour
1/4 cup arrowroot flour
1 tsp baking powder (see recipe below)
1/2 tsp sea salt
1 tbsp olive oil or avocado oil
1/4 cup coconut milk mixed with 1 tsp lemon juice (or coconut yogurt)
3/4 cup hot water
1 tbsp more olive oil or avocado oil

Baking powder recipe:
2 tablespoons cream of tartar
1 tablespoon baking soda
1 tablespoon arrowroot powder
Mix everything well in a parchment paper and then transfer to an air-tight powder.

Method:

In a large mixing bowl add the flours, baking powder and salt. Mix using a fork. Then add the oil, coconut milk lemon mixture (or coconut yogurt). Mix lightly to form a crumbly mixture.

Then add the hot water in 2 or 3 portions mixing with a spoon after each addition. After all the water is added, again mix well to make sure all the flour is wet.

Wait for a couple minutes for the mixture to cool a bit and then knead using your hands to form a smooth dough. Add the extra oil to the dough and knead again for 2-3 minutes until the dough gets really soft and smooth. Divide the dough into 8 equal size balls. Cover the bowl with a dish.

Take a ball of dough and roll it on a rolling board or on parchment paper using a rolling pin to about 1/4 inch thickness.

Heat a cast iron or non stick pan until hot. Turn heat to medium and then place the rolled out naan onto the pan. Cook on medium heat for 1 minute and flip using a spatula. Cook for about 2 minutes and then flip again.

Now press the naan from all the sides using the spatula and while you do that, the naan will begin to puff up. Remove from the pan and transfer to a plate.

Continue cooking all the rest of the naans the same way.

Naan with Yeast

This was one of my first successful naan recipes. The plantain flour makes it quite delicious! If you don't have plantain flour, you can use green plantain puree or you can just use more cassava flour. You can cook these on the stove top or also bake them in the oven!

Serves: 2-3

Ingredients:
1/4 cup warm water
1 tsp maple syrup
1/2 tbsp dry active yeast
3/4 cup cassava flour
1/4 cup plantain flour (if you don't have plantain flour, you can use 1/4 cup green plantain puree or use more cassava flour)
1/2 tsp sea salt
3/4 cup warm water (use half cup water if using plantain puree above)
1-2 tbsp extra virgin olive oil

Method:
In a cup or a small bowl, add the warm water (water should be between 80 and 90 deg F) and the maple syrup. Then add the yeast and stir with a spoon to let the yeast completely dissolve/mix into the water. Cover with an inverted cup or a dish and keep aside for about 10-15 minutes until the yeast gets activated and gets all bubbly and rises to almost double its volume.

Take a large glass mixing bowl and add the cassava flour and the plantain flours (if not adding plantain flour, just add plantain puree all the cassava flour) to it. Add the sea salt too. Now add the yeast mixture (risen by now) and stir to mix.

Add the rest of the warm water and mix with a spatula to form a dough. Cover the bowl with a kitchen towel and place a dish on top and leave aside for about 1 to 2 hours (1 1/2 hours is perfect!) (If the room temperature is less than 70 F, then keep the dough inside an oven with the oven lights on).

To the fermented dough, add a tbsp of extra virgin olive oil and knead gently (don't knead too much) until smooth. Divide dough into about 6 balls.

On a parchment paper take each ball and flatten using your fingers to form a 3 inch diameter round circle(or an oval naan shape). The thickness should be about least 1/4 of an inch. If its too thin, then it will be like a tortilla. Heat a non stick pan or a cast iron pan until hot. Then cook the naan on the pan for about 2-3 minutes on each side on medium heat. Brush with some olive oil on each side. Finish cooking all the naans this way.

Baking Naans in oven:
Line a baking tray with parchment paper. Take each ball of dough and press onto the parchment to form a 3 inch diameter naan. Place about 2 -3 naan on tray and bake at 375 F for 12 minutes on one side and then flip and apply oil on the other side and cook for another 5 minutes.

Cauliflower Paratha

Parathas are flatbreads which are cooked with oil or ghee. And vegetables are usually mixed with the dough too. This cauliflower paratha is absolutely delicious and you can have it just like that!

Serves: 2-3

Ingredients:

2 cups cauliflower florets (about 1/2 of a large cauliflower)
1/2 tsp sea salt
About 1 cup cassava flour
About 1/2 cup water
1 tbsp of extra virgin olive oil
Additional extra virgin olive oil for topping the naans

Method:

Steam the cauliflower florets using a steamer. (You can also boil them with 1/2 cup of water for about 5 minutes.) If boiling, drain the boiled water completely before mashing.

Place the steamed (or boiled) cauliflower in a mixing bowl and mash it completely using a potato masher till you get a smooth puree. Add the salt and mix.

Add the cassava flour and start to knead using your hands. Add the water slowly in portions (you may need less or more water depending upon how much water is in your cauliflower) until you get a dough. Add the oil to make the dough smooth.

If dough is still sticky, add 1-2 tbsp of additional cassava flour till you get a smooth dough. Divide dough into 6 balls.

Heat a cast iron or non stick pan on medium heat for 5 minutes.

Meanwhile roll one dough ball between parchment papers into a round shape of about 4 inches diameter and about 1/2 inch thickness.

Transfer the paratha onto the hot pan. Let cook for 1 minute and then flip to the other side. Let cook for 2 minutes on this side and flip it back to the other side again and cook for another 30 seconds before transferring to a dish. Apply some olive oil on top. Repeat process with all the other dough balls. Serve parathas warm.

Sweet Potato Paratha

I love both the texture and flavor of this sweet potato paratha. It can also be made into a thicker flatbread and used for making sandwiches.

Serves: 2-3

Ingredients:

1/2 cup plus 2 tbsp cassava flour
2 tbsp arrow root flour
1/4 tsp sea salt
3/4 cup cooked and mashed white sweet potato
1-2 tbsp extra cassava flour (if needed)
1 tbsp olive oil or avocado oil
About 2- 3 tbsp extra oil for pan frying

Method:

In a large mixing bowl, add the flours and the salt and mix using a spatula. Then add the mashed sweet potato.

Using your hands mix everything and knead to form a dough. If the dough is too sticky (depends on how much water is in your mashed sweet potato), add extra cassava flour as needed till you get a non sticky smooth dough.

Add the oil and knead further to make it soft and smooth. Divide dough into 8 dough balls. Cover the dough balls with a dish cloth or a lid.

Place a cast iron pan or skillet to heat.
While the pan is heating, take each dough ball and roll between parchment paper sheets using a rolling pin to form a circle about 1/4 inch thick (about 3.5" to 4 " diameter circle).

When the pan is hot, turn heat to medium and transfer the rolled paratha onto the pan.

Cook for 2 minutes and then flip to the other side. Apply about 1/2 a tsp of oil on the flipped surface. Cook for about 1 minute and then again flip to the other side. Apply 1/4 tsp of oil on this side as well and cook for 30 seconds more or until this side has a few brown spots. Transfer to a dish and keep warm with a kitchen towel.

Repeat this process until all the dough balls are cooked.
Serve parathas warm. Left over parathas can be placed in refrigerator for 2-3 days or in freezer for a month.

Appam (Lacy Crepes)

Appams are a traditional gluten free, fermented flat bread made with rice flour and yeast. The loose batter will form bubbles when poured into the hot pan and that gives it the characteristic lacy look!

Serves: 2-3

Ingredients:

1/4 cup warm water
1 tsp yeast
1 tsp coconut sugar
1/2 cup cassava flour
1 tbsp coconut flour
1/4 tsp sea salt
1/4 cup coconut milk
1 cup water, in 2 divided portions
1/2 cup sparkling water (Pellegrino)
About 1/4 cup coconut oil for making the crepes

Method:

In a large mixing bowl add the warm water (it should be around 80 – 90 F) , the yeast and the sugar and mix well. Cover with a dish cloth and leave aside for 5 minutes.

Once the yeast mixture becomes foamy, add the two flours, the salt and the coconut milk. Using a spatula mix everything well together until you get a wet thick doughy mixture.

Now add 1/2 of the water and again mix until you get a thick but pourable mixture. Cover with a dish cloth and a lid and keep aside to ferment for anywhere between 2 to 10 hours.

When you are ready to make the crepes, heat a stainless steel or cast iron skillet until hot.
To the cassava mixture, add the sparkling water and mix well.

Brush the hot skillet with coconut oil and lower heat to medium.

Pour about 1/2 a cup of the batter into the pan and immediately twirl the pan slightly to help spread the batter. The bubbles formed in the batter will give it the lacy look.

Let the crepe cook for about 2 minutes on medium heat and then carefully using a spatula flip the crepe to the other side. Let cook for 2 more minutes. Transfer to a serving plate.

Repeat the process using the rest of the batter. As you make crepes, remember to let cool them first completely before piling on top of each other as the crepes will stick to each other when hot.

VEGETABLE SIDES

'Nutrient density' is an important focus of AIP. It is not just enough to avoid inflammatory foods but it is equally important to eat nutrient dense foods and vegetables are an important category when it comes to nutrient dense foods. Rotating your vegetables is very important too, so you can maximize the amount of nutrients your body can get.

In an effort to keep it simple and easy for my clients, I usually recommend roasting and batch cooking vegetables. That is definitely a great way to eat more vegetables. Steaming and sautéing are also great options. You can use any combination of AIP approved seasonings. In this section, I wanted to include my different recipes for vegetables that are based on traditional Indian recipes. These recipes helped me to continue to eat vegetables without getting bored!

The Vegetable coconut stew is a great recipe for batch cooking and it is also quite filling. So just a piece of fish or chicken on the side and a large bowl of this stew is enough to keep you satiated for a while!

This section also includes 'cauliflower pilaf', cassava 'rice' and yogurt 'rice' which are great 'rice' options to pair with curries and stews. I have also included simple vegetable dishes cooked with coconut which is a very traditional southern Indian way of cooking vegetables. Creamy mashed Cassava is another good starchy side dish that goes wonderfully with seafood and chicken curries. You will also find a couple appetizer dishes like 'onion pakoras' and 'green plantain fritters' thrown in here since I consider them as a 'side' to be paired with other vegetables and proteins.

Aloo Gobhi

Aloo Gobhi is a quintessential Indian vegetable dish with cauliflower and potatoes and you will find it in most Indian restaurants. But the best one is the one made at home! In this AIP version, I use white sweet potatoes instead of regular potatoes and the slight sweetness actually makes this dish even better!

Serves: 2

Ingredients:

2 tbsp extra virgin olive oil
1/2 of a medium red onion, thinly sliced
1 tsp fresh ginger, grated
6-8 fresh curry leaves torn apart (use dried curry leaves if fresh is not available)
1/2 tsp sea salt
1/2 tsp turmeric powder
1 medium size white sweet potato, peeled and diced into 1/2 inch cubes
1/4 cup water
1/2 of a medium head of cauliflower, cut into florets, about 2 cups
1/4 cup fresh cilantro leaves with tender stalks, chopped up
1 tbsp lemon juice

Method:

Heat a stainless steel skillet and when hot add the oil. Turn heat to medium and add the onions. Saute for two minutes. Then add the ginger and curry leaves and saute for 1 more minute.

Then add the salt, turmeric and the sweet potato cubes. Stir fry to coat the sweet potato with the spices. Cover and cook for 5 minutes on low heat.

Open lid and add the water and add the cauliflower and stir everything to mix. Cover and cook again for 3-4 minutes until the sweet potato is cooked all the way through and the cauliflower is just soft. Turn heat off and add the cilantro and lemon juice and stir. Serve warm.

Reintroduction Notes: *You can add 1/2 tsp cumin seeds and 1/2 tsp fennel seeds (both stage 1 reintroduction foods) to the oil before adding the onions.*

Vegetable Coconut Stew (Avial)

Avial is a traditional Keralan dish made from a variety of vegetables cooked and smothered in a sauce made with coconut and some spices. The fresh curry leaves and extra virgin coconut oil provide a lot of flavor to this dish. It is a very satiating dish owing to the starchy carbs and hence great when you are initially starting on AIP.

Serves: 4-6

Ingredients:

1 green plantain, scraped to remove strings and chopped into 1 inch long pieces (no need to remove skin)
3 medium size taro root, skin scraped and cut into 1 inch cubes
2 cups of water
2 tsp salt
About 1 cup carrots cut up into 1 inch long and 1/4 inch wide pieces
2 small zucchini, cut up into 1 inch long and 1/2 inch wide pieces
Yellow squash, cut into 1 inch cubes, about 1 cup
Acorn squash, peeled and cut into 1/2 inch cubes, about 1/2 cup
1 medium red onion, cut into long, thin slices
1 tsp turmeric powder
1 small piece of tamarind (about the size of a quarter) or 1 small piece of Kodampuli

For the ground masala paste:
1 1/2 cups grated coconut (fresh or frozen coconut pieces or freshly grated or frozen grated or shredded coconut) -if using frozen, thaw beforehand
1/2 cup hot water
1/4 tsp turmeric powder
2 cloves of garlic, peeled
2 tbsp coconut yogurt or coconut milk
1 tbsp lemon juice

For garnish:
2 tbsp extra virgin coconut oil
6-8 fresh curry leaves (with stem preferably)

Method:

Take a big cooking pot which is wide and has a tight-fitting lid. First add the hard vegetables (green plantain and taro) along with 2 cups of water and the salt and cook uncovered for about a minute till the water starts boiling and then cover and cook on medium flame for about 3-4 minutes till the vegetables are a little soft.

Next add the rest of the vegetables and the onion and cook covered on medium heat for another 2-3 minutes until the vegetables are about 80% cooked.

Open and stir and add about 1/4 cup more water. Also add the turmeric, and the piece of tamarind (or kodampuli) at this point and again cover and cook for another two minutes.

Stir to make sure the veggies are not sticking to the bottom of the pot. Turn heat off.

Now, to make the coconut masala, add all the ingredients listed under 'For the ground masala paste' into a blender/food processor jar and blend for about 30 seconds till you get a coarsely ground paste.

Add the coconut yogurt/coconut milk and blend again till smooth for another 15 seconds.

Add this paste to the pot with the vegetables and stir slowly and carefully trying not to mash the vegetables too much.

Finally, put the pot back on the stove turning the heat to low and add the fresh curry leaves and the coconut oil and mix lightly.

Reintroduction Notes:
You can add 1/2 tsp cumin seeds (stage 1 reintroduction) to the ground masala ingredients.

Zucchini Barta (Roasted Mashed Zucchini)

I used to love eggplants and so I created this AIP version of Baingan (Eggplant) barta using zucchinis. Roasting the zucchini along with the onions and garlic is what gives this dish its delicious, smoky flavor. This can be served as a dip with plantain chips or with some flatbread!

Serves: 2-4

Ingredients:

1 tsp avocado oil
2 medium size zucchini, whole
1 small red onion, roughly chopped
4 large garlic cloves, unpeeled
1/2 tsp sea salt
1/2 cup fresh cilantro leaves
1 tbsp lime juice
1 tbsp extra virgin olive oil

Method:

Pre heat oven to 400 F.
Line a medium size baking sheet with Aluminium foil and brush lightly with the avocado oil.

Place the whole zucchinis, the onions and the whole garlic cloves on the baking sheet. Brush the vegetables too with the oil and place the tray in the oven on the bottom rack. Bake for 15 minutes. Remove the garlic cloves out and squeeze the roasted garlic puree out from the garlic and transfer to a small bowl and keep aside.

Now turn the oven to Broil setting. And move the tray to the top rack about 6-8 inches from the broiler. Broil for about 1 minute. Turn oven off and get the tray out.

Let the roasted vegetables cool for about 5 minutes. In a food processor, add the roasted zucchini, the onions and the garlic puree. Add the salt, cilantro and lime juice and blend for 30 seconds till smooth. Transfer to a serving bowl and drizzle the olive oil on top.

Kale with Coconut

In southern Indian cuisine, it is a common practice to use fresh grated coconut in most vegetable dishes. The garlic and the bacon fat make this dish additionally flavorful.

Serves: 3-4

Ingredients:

4 cups finely chopped kale leaves
1 tbsp coconut oil
1 tsp bacon fat
2 large garlic cloves, finely chopped
1/4 tsp sea salt
1/4 tsp turmeric
1/4 cup shredded coconut

Method:

Wash the Kale leaves and place on a strainer to drain the water.

Heat a large stainless steel skillet. Add the coconut oil and the bacon fat.

When the oil is hot, add the garlic and stir fry for 30 seconds on medium heat.

Next add the washed Kale leaves. Also add the salt and turmeric and stir fry to mix. Cover skillet with a lid and lower heat to low. Cook on low heat for about 8-10 minutes or until the kale leaves are really soft (and not chewy). Turn heat off and add the shredded coconut and mix well.

***Reintroduction Notes:** You can add 1/2 tsp cumin seeds (stage 1 reintroduction) to the oil along with the garlic.*

Creamy Mashed Cassava

Mashed cassava is a common starchy side in Kerala cuisine and is often paired with beef *(See Kerala Beef Bowl under 'Curryto Bowls' on page 152)*

Serves: 2

Ingredients:

1/2 lb. cassava root, peeled and cut up into 1 inch cubes (about 2 cups) - you can use fresh or frozen cassava root
1/2 tsp sea salt
Enough water to immerse the cassava pieces completely
2 tbsp extra virgin coconut oil, melted
1 tbsp shallot or red onions, finely chopped
1 tbsp finely minced garlic
1 tsp grated fresh ginger
1/4 tsp turmeric powder
6-8 fresh curry leaves
1/4 cup shredded coconut or frozen grated coconut (that has been thawed to room temperature)

Method:

In a large cooking pot, add the cassava pieces along with the salt and add enough water to immerse all the cassava pieces completely. Place pot on stove and heat until the water starts boiling. Then turn heat to low and cover the pot leaving a slight opening. Cook for about 15-20 minutes until the cassava is tender and cooked all the way through. Check periodically throughout the cooking period to make sure there is enough water and adding more water if necessary.

Turn heat off. Strain through a strainer to drain the excess cooking water reserving about 1/4 of the water. Add the reserved water back to the pot with the cassava and using a potato masher, mash the cassava completely while it is hot. Keep aside.

In a small pan or sauce pan, heat the coconut oil. When hot, add the shallots (or the onions) and saute for 2 minutes on medium heat until they turn golden. Then add the garlic, the ginger, turmeric and the curry leaves.

Stir fry for another 30 seconds and turn heat off. Pour this flavored oil mixture onto the mashed cassava. Add the coconut too and mix everything well together. Serve warm.

Masala Okra with Bacon

Okra is filled with nutrients. It is also really delicious and I like it both crisp and mushy. In this recipe, you need to cook it such that it retains a crisp texture and not get mushy. The bacon, of course is what makes this dish a fusion dish!

Serves: 2

Ingredients:

1 strip of bacon, chopped into small pieces
2 cups frozen okra, thawed
1/4 tsp sea salt
1/2 tsp AIP Curry powder (see recipe on page 221)
4-6 fresh curry leaves (optional)

Method:

In a large stainless steel skillet, add the bacon bits and cook on low heat till they get crisp (about 4-5 minutes). To the same pan, add the okra and the salt . Stir fry for 1 minute and then cover and cook for 5 minutes on low heat.

Open the lid and add the curry powder and fresh curry leaves. Stir to mix and continue to cook uncovered on low to medium heat for 8-10 minutes more until the okra get crisp. Keep stirring every two minutes or so to avoid burning the spices.

Onion Pakoras

These crispy onion pakoras are a great appetizer or a side to any meal! They remind me of cold, rainy days when my mom would make them for evening tea!

Serves: 2-3

Ingredients:

1 of a medium red onion, thinly sliced
1/2 cup cassava flour
1/4 cup singoda flour / water chestnut flour (or tiger nut flour)
1/4 tsp sea salt
1/2 tsp turmeric
1/4 cup plus 2 tbsp water
About 1 cup coconut oil or avocado oil for deep frying

Method:

In a large mixing bowl, add the onions, the flours, salt and turmeric. Use your hands to crush the onions into the flour and spice mixture. Do this for a couple minutes until the flour gets a bit wet from the juices released from the onions.

Now slowly add the water bit by bit till you get a sticky dough. (It should not be too watery it should be just sticky - you may not need to use the entire quantity of water)

In a deep skillet or kadai (a wok shaped pan) heat the oil for deep frying. Heat the oil for about 4 to 5 minutes until the oil gets hot. Then turn heat between medium and low setting.

Now make small balls out of the dough mixture using your hands and add into the hot oil (You could also use a spoon to do this)

Fry the pakoras in batches on medium heat for about 2-3 minutes and then flip them over and fry for another 1-2 minutes until brown and crispy (take care not to burn them).

Transfer to a dish lined with paper towel to catch the extra oil. Serve pakoras warm with cilantro or mint chutney.

Cassava 'Rice'

This 'rice' recipe is a traditional southern Indian breakfast dish called 'Puttu'. This goes fabulously with all curries - be it chicken, fish or beef!

Serves: 2-3

Ingredients:

1 cup cassava flour
1/4 tsp sea salt
1/2 cup fresh grated/shredded coconut
About 1/2 cup water (if using dried shredded coconut, add 2 tbsp more)
1/4 cup extra grated coconut or shredded coconut for the base

Method:

In a large mixing bowl, add the flour, sea salt and the coconut. Mix lightly and then slowly add the water in portions and mix using your hands to wet the flour. Use your fingers to form a crumbly mixture. Continue adding the water until the mixture is completely moist and there are large lumps but stop adding water before it can form a dough. The mixture should come together into a ball when you press it inside your fist but the ball should be crumbly and break easily.

Pour about 1 cup water into a large cooking pot (that can fit a steamer on the top) and let it come to a boil. Then turn heat to medium.

In a steamer basket / flat strainer, spread some shredded coconut on the bottom and then spread the cassava mixture on top (You may have to do this in batches depending upon the size of your pot).

Now place this steamer vessel on top of the pot such that it doesn't touch the water. Cover the steamer and the pot using a lid that fits well (without letting steam escape).

Cook for about 10 minutes and then turn heat off. Take steamer insert out and carefully invert onto a dish. Break the soft cake using a fork to get cassava 'rice'.

Note: You can also use an Instant Pot to steam the cassava mixture.

Green Plantain Fritters (Vadas)

These scrumptious green plantain 'vadas' are deep fried and flavored with cilantro and ginger. They are perfect for an appetizer or a snack!

Serves: 2-3

Ingredients:

For the filling:
1 large green plantain (very green and unripe)
1/2 cup packed fresh cilantro leaves
1/2 inch by 1/2 inch piece of fresh ginger
1 tsp lemon juice
1/2 tsp sea salt
1/2 tsp turmeric

For the coating batter:
2 tbsp cassava flour
1 tbsp water chestnut flour (singoda flour) or tiger nut flour
1/4 tsp turmeric powder
1/4 tsp sea salt
6 tbsp water
About 1/2 cup coconut oil for frying

Method:

In a medium size cooking pot, place the green plantain (cut in half or 3 pieces) with skin on. Add enough water to submerge the pieces completely. Cover with a lid placing it slightly ajar and cook on medium heat for about 12-15 minutes until the plantain is completely cooked from the inside.

Making the balls:
Remove the skin from the cooked plantains and place the plantains in a bowl taking care not to add any water. While hot, mash the plantains completely using a potato masher. Leave it aside to cool.

In a food processor, add all the rest of the filling ingredients and process it for 30 seconds till you get a coarse paste. Now add the paste to the mashed plantains and mix well using a spoon. Divide this dough into 8 equal size balls.

To make the batter:
Mix all batter ingredients except the water in a bowl and then add the water slowly to form a thick pasty mixture.

Deep frying the balls:
In a small frying pan, add the coconut oil and heat for 2-3 minutes on medium heat until hot. Now dip each ball into the coating batter and coat it completely and then place balls one by one gently in the oil. Deep fry till they are golden brown on the outside. drain on paper towels.

Cauliflower Pilaf

This pilaf recipe is simple however just the use of a couple spices elevates it to a dish that is so much more special than just cauliflower 'rice'! Try it!

Serves: 2

Ingredients:

1 tbsp coconut oil
1 bay leaf
1 one inch piece of cinnamon stick
2 cups cauliflower rice (fresh or frozen)
1/4 tsp sea salt
1/2 tsp turmeric powder
8-10 saffron strands mixed with 2 tbsp warm coconut milk (optional)
1 tbsp fresh cilantro, chopped fine

Method:

Heat a medium size sauce pan and add the coconut oil. Add the bay leaf and the cinnamon. Stir for 30 seconds and then add the cauliflower rice.

Add the salt and turmeric and stir to mix everything well. Cover the sauce pan with a tight fitting lid and cook on low heat for 3-4 minutes (longer if using frozen cauliflower rice) until the cauliflower rice is well-cooked and soft.

Turn heat off. Add the saffron coconut milk mixture (if adding) and cilantro and mix well.

Green Papaya Thoran

'Thoran' is a generic name for any vegetable side which uses shredded coconut. This same recipe can be used for cabbage too using shredded cabbage instead of grated green papaya.

Serves: 2 -3

Ingredients:

1 tbsp coconut oil
5-6 fresh or dried curry leaves
1 tbsp finely chopped shallot
1 tbsp finely chopped garlic
3 cups, grated green papaya (skin peeled)
1/2 tsp sea salt
1/4 tsp turmeric
1/2 cup frozen grated coconut that has been thawed to room temperature (or shredded coconut)

Method:

Take a medium size pan and heat the coconut oil in it. Then add the curry leaves and turn heat to medium. Add the onions and garlic and stir fry for about 30 seconds.

Now add the grated papaya, salt and turmeric. Stir to mix everything well and cover with a lid.

Cook on low heat for about 5 minutes until the green papaya is 75% cooked but still has a slight bite to it. Turn heat off and add the grated/shredded coconut.

Reintroduction Notes: *You can add 1/2 tsp mustard seeds and 1/2 tsp cumin seeds (stage 1 reintroductions) to the hot oil before adding the shallots.*

Yogurt 'Rice'

Yogurt rice or 'curd' rice as it's called is a typical comfort food of southern India and is made when you want a light fare for dinner or lunch or it is usually consumed towards the end of a large meal as it helps with digestion.

Serves: 2

Ingredients:

1 tbsp coconut oil
2 cups fresh or frozen cauliflower rice (thawed if frozen)
1 tbsp water
1/4 tsp sea salt
1 tsp fresh grated ginger
4-6 fresh curry leaves
1 tbsp fresh cilantro leaves, chopped fine
1/4 cup coconut yogurt (for homemade, see recipe on page 226; if you do not have coconut yogurt, you can use coconut milk)
1 tsp lemon juice
1 tbsp finely chopped radish (optional)
extra sea salt if needed

Method:

Heat a small sauce pan and add the coconut oil. Then add the cauliflower rice, water and the salt. Stir and cover and cook on low heat for about 5 to 7 minutes until the 'rice' turns soft. Turn heat off and keep aside to cool.

Take a mixing bowl and add the ginger, curry leaves, cilantro and yogurt (or coconut milk), lemon juice and the radish (if adding). Stir using a spoon and then add the cooled cauliflower rice to the bowl.

Stir gently to mix the rice with all the yogurt mixture. Check for seasoning and add additional salt if needed.

CHUTNEYS AND ACCOMPANIMENTS

One of the unique features of Indian cuisine is that it has a plethora of chutneys and pickles (relishes). These accompaniments are served in mini servings alongside the main dishes and help to elevate the meal. Chutneys are made from a lot of different foods - coconut, nuts and vegetables. Pickles are usually extremely spicy and sour and have spices that help digestion like ginger and asafoetida. Lemon and green mangoes are very commonly used for making pickles.

I make big batches of the cilantro and mint chutney and freeze them in ice cube molds. That way when I feel like adding a chutney to my meal, I just need to thaw a couple pieces! Tamarind chutney is another favorite and a little drizzle of it does wonders to your meal! It also doubles up as a bbq sauce and is super easy to make too!

Raita is a yogurt dish that is very cooling and helps to balance out the strong spicy flavors in curries and stews. The AIP raita is pretty good and it can be made instantly!

Since AIP excludes many of the spices that I was used to, I started creating AIP versions of pickles which helped to tickle my taste buds even when I was eating a non spicy food. These chutneys and pickles just add variety and make even the simplest of meals a bit more interesting!

Apple Chutney

This sweet, spicy and tangy chutney made from apples and dates is a perfect complement to steaming hot parathas! And is a great side to any meal!

Serves: 3-4

Ingredients:

2 medium size apples, peeled and chopped
(Use a soft cooking variety like macintosh)
4 dates, pitted and chopped
1 tbsp lemon juice
1/2 inch piece of fresh ginger, chopped fine
1/4 tsp cinnamon powder
1/4 tsp salt
1 tbsp coconut sugar
1/2 cup water

Method:

Add all the ingredients to a medium size cooking pot. Place on the stove on medium heat. After 1 minute, cover with a lid and reduce heat to low and let simmer for about 10 minutes. (Stir occasionally to avoid any burning).

Now open the lid - the apple and date pieces should have softened. (If not, again cook for about 5 more minutes).

Once the apples are all mushy, cook uncovered for another 5 minutes or so on low simmer until the mixture thickens and resembles a nice thick chutney/spread consistency.

Chutney can stay outside at room temperature for about 4 days and in the refrigerator for up to 10 days.

Lemon Pickle

Indian Pickles are actually relishes that are usually quite spicy and sour. Lemon pickles are also excellent for digestion because of the bitter oils in them. I used to love them so much that I had to create an AIP version!

Serves: 4-6

Ingredients:

2 tbsp olive oil
2 organic lemon, cut into small pieces
1 inch by 1 inch piece of fresh ginger, peeled and chopped fine
1/2 tsp turmeric
4-6 fresh curry leaves
2 tsp sea salt
1/4 tsp asafoetida
2 tbsp apple cider vinegar

Method:

Heat the olive oil in a small sauce pan. Add the cut lemon pieces, the fresh ginger, turmeric, curry leaves and salt. Cover and cook for 3 minutes. Open and add the asafetida and the apple cider vinegar. Stir to mix and turn heat off.

You can use this pickle immediately or you can store it in an air tight container and use it after 7 days or until the lemon rind gets softer.

Coconut Chutney

Coconut chutney is an important item in a south Indian menu and it complements rice as well as breads. This is one of the simplest versions that my mom used to make. I only had to exclude the green chillies to make it AIP compliant.

Serves: 2-3

Ingredients:

1 cup frozen grated coconut, thawed to room temperature (or dry shredded coconut)
1/4 of a small red onion or a shallot
1/2 inch by 1/2 inch piece of fresh ginger, peeled
1/4 tsp sea salt
3-4 fresh curry leaves (optional)
1 tbsp lemon or lime juice
1/4 cup warm water (use hot water if using shredded coconut)

For garnish:
1 tbsp coconut oil
4-6 fresh curry leaves

Method:

In a small food processor jar, add all the ingredients and blend until smooth. Transfer to a serving bowl.

In a small pan, heat the coconut oil. Add the fresh curry leaves and stir fry for 2 minutes until they turn crisp. Pour this oil mixture onto the chutney and stir.

Cilantro Coconut Chutney

Cilantro coconut chutney is a variation of the coconut chutney. The added ginger and lemon makes this chutney finger-licking delicious!

Serves: 2-3

Ingredients:

1 cup (packed) fresh cilantro leaves (big stems removed)
1 inch by 1 inch piece of fresh ginger, peeled
1 tbsp fresh lemon juice
1/4 tsp sea salt
1/2 cup fresh frozen grated coconut or dried shredded coconut
1/4 cup hot water

Method:

Place all the ingredients in a small food processor jar and blend till you get a very fine and smooth texture. Transfer to a serving bowl.

Notes:
1. If using shredded coconut, rehydrate by soaking it in a bowl with the hot water first for about 10 minutes before blending.
2. The chutney tastes best fresh and can stay in the refrigerator for 2 days.
3. The chutney freezes well too and I like to freeze them in tiny silicone molds or in ice cube trays.

Red Onion Pickle

This pickle / relish is great with grilled chicken or fish. And also on salads. The radish is optional however I like the combo as the radish gives it a spiciness. I like to use a mandolin slicer to slice the onions and the radish.

Serves: 2-4

Ingredients:

1 medium red onion, thinly sliced
1 small radish, thinly sliced (optional)
1/4 tsp sea salt
1 tbsp extra virgin coconut oil, melted
1 tbsp apple cider vinegar or lime juice

Method:

Mix all the ingredients together in a small bowl. Using your hands, scrunch the onions a bit. Leave aside for 5 minutes.

Pickle is ready to serve and can be stored in the refrigerator for 2-3 days.

Ginger Chutney

This sweet and spicy chutney is great for digestion as well as for stirring up your appetite. Due to these reasons, this chutney is an important component of the elaborate 'sadya' or traditional feast!

Serves: 4-6

Ingredients:
2 tbsp coconut oil
1/2 cup of grated fresh ginger
4-6 fresh curry leaves (or dried curry leaves)
A ping pong ball size of tamarind soaked in 1/4 cup hot water for 10 minutes (or 1 tbsp tamarind extract mixed with 1/4 cup water)
1/4 tsp sea salt
1 tbsp coconut sugar

Method:
If using tamarind, then press the tamarind using your hands to form a pulp.

Strain through a strainer to get the extract. Keep aside. If using tamarind extract, mix it with the water and keep aside.

In a stainless steel skillet, add the oil and when hot, turn heat to medium and add the ginger and the curry leaves. Stir fry for 4-5 minutes on medium heat.

Now add the tamarind water, salt and coconut sugar. Let simmer for 4-5 minutes or until all the water is evaporated and you get a thick consistency. Turn heat off and let cool.

You can use the chutney as is or you can blend it in a food processor to get a paste like consistency. Store in refrigerator for up to 2 weeks.

Tamarind Chutney (aka BBQ Sauce)

This is a chutney you would want to drizzle over pretty much anything and everything! Tangy, sweet and spicy! Also perfect as a bbq sauce!

Serves: 6-8

Ingredients:

1/4 cup tamarind paste soaked in 1/2 cup hot water (or 2 tbsp tamarind extract mixed with 1/2 cup water)
1 tsp ground ginger
1/4 tsp sea salt
1/4 cup unsulfured molasses

Method:

If using tamarind, then press the tamarind using your hands to form a pulp. Strain through a strainer to get the extract. If using ready made tamarind extract, mix it with the water.

Add the tamarind extract to a sauce pan along with the rest of the ingredients and cook on low heat for about 8-10 minutes (stirring frequently)until you get a thick sauce. Turn heat off and let cool.
Transfer to an air-tight container and let it sit at room temperature for about a week or in the refrigerator for up to 1 month.

Green Mango and Olive Pickle

Green Olives give a twist to this traditional green mango pickle! My cousin shared her recipe me with me and I couldn't wait to try making an AIP version since I love olives! If green mangoes are not in season, you can use a less ripe regular mango for a sweet and sour pickle.

Serves: 4-6

Ingredients:

2 tbsp extra virgin olive oil
6 large garlic cloves, peeled and thinly sliced
6-8 fresh curry leaves (optional)
1 medium size green mango, peeled and cut up into tiny pieces (about 1/4 inch by 1/4 inch), about 1 cup
1/4 tsp turmeric
1/2 tsp sea salt
1/4 tsp asafoetida powder (make sure it is gluten free)
1/2 cup organic pitted green olives or kalamata olives (make sure to use an AIP compliant brand), chopped up
Extra 1 tbsp extra virgin olive oil.

Method:

Heat a small stainless steel sauce pan. When hot, turn heat to medium and add the olive oil.

Add the garlic and the curry leaves and stir fry for 30 seconds. Then add the mango pieces, turmeric, salt and asafoetida. Stir to mix and cover and cook for 5 to 7 minutes until the mango turns soft.

Add in the olives and stir. Drizzle the additional extra virgin olive oil on top. Let cool and transfer to an air tight container.

The pickle can stay at room temperature for up to a week and in the refrigerator for a month.

Raita

Raita is a yogurt dish that is very cooling and complements hot and spicy dishes.

Serves: 2

Ingredients:

1/2 of an English cucumber, peeled and chopped fine
1/2 of a medium size red onion, chopped fine
1/2 cup coconut yogurt (or coconut milk)
1 tsp lemon juice
1/8 tsp rock salt or sea salt

Method:

Mix all the ingredients in a small bowl. Keep in the refrigerator until served.

Mint (Pudina) Chutney

This spicy mint chutney is great to give a burst of flavor to any simple dish! In summer, I like to make a big batch and freeze it in ice cube molds.

Serves: 3-6

Ingredients:

3 cups fresh mint leaves (no stems)
1 cup fresh cilantro leaves
1/2 tsp Black salt or Kala Namak (can substitute with sea salt)
1/4 tsp Aamchur or dry mango powder (optional)
1 inch by 1 inch piece of fresh ginger, peeled and chopped up roughly
Juice of 1 lemon (about 2 tbsp)
1 tbsp water

Method:

In a food processor or a blender jar, add all the ingredients and blend everything till you get a thick pasty mixture (make sure there are no chunks of ginger left). Transfer to a clean dry glass jar.

This chutney can stay in the refrigerator for up to a week. Or you can pour the chutney into ice cube molds or silicone molds and freeze for up to 3 months.

SALADS

I decided to include this section only to show different salads that are unique to Indian cuisine. The four different salads here will add to your salad repertoire! And we all know how important that is when you are AIP-ing!

The Broccoli sprouts salad is one of my favorites and I make it frequently sprouting broccoli sprouts using my sprouter.

The fruit chaat salad can be an accompaniment to a meal or you can just eat it as a snack or even as dessert!

Fruit Chaat

Sweet, Spicy, Sour and Salty - all of these four taste sensations are what you get in a fruit chaat! Some tangy and some sweet fruits sprinkled with a spicy dry masala mix! So yum!

Serves: 2

Ingredients:

1 cup chopped kiwis
1 cup chopped mango
1 tsp AIP Chaat masala (recipe on page 224)
1 tsp fresh mint (or dried mint) finely chopped

Method:

Mix all the ingredients in a bowl and place in the refrigerator for a few minutes before serving!

Note:
You can use any combination of fruits.

Kachumber Salad

This salad uses fresh grated vegetables like radish and cucumber with lemon juice as the dressing!

Serves: 2

Ingredients:

1/2 cup grated radish
1/2 cup grated cucumber
1/2 cup grated carrot
1/2 of a small red onion thinly sliced
2 tbsp lime/lemon juice
1/4 tsp black salt /kala Namak (substitute with sea salt)
2 tbsp chopped fresh cilantro

Method:

Add all ingredients to a serving bowl. Mix everything well using a fork. Keep aside for 5-10 minutes before serving!

Broccoli Sprouts Salad

Broccoli sprouts are power packed with nutrients and this salad is a delicious way to get those nutrients in!

Serves: 2

Ingredients:
2 cups of broccoli sprouts
1 small size cucumber peeled and diced
1/2 of a small red onion, finely sliced or chopped
1/8 tsp sea salt
1 tsp lemon juice
1/2 tsp AIP chaat masala (recipe on page 224)

Method:

Mix all ingredients together in a salad bowl and serve immediately!

Cabbage and Pineapple Salad

This salad is one of my dad's special recipes that he used to always make whenever we had guests over for dinner. I had not made it in a while and this recipe came to memory as I was testing recipes for this book! This recipe tastes best when let to sit overnight.

Serves: 2

Ingredients:

1/3rd of a medium cabbage, shredded finely
1 cup pineapple, chopped (sliced into 1 inch or longer pieces)
1/4 tsp sea salt
1/4 tsp ground ginger
1 tbsp apple cider vinegar

Method:

Mix all the ingredients in a bowl and let sit for anywhere between 2 hours to overnight in the refrigerator.

Mix well again before serving to mix the juices.

ESSENTIALS

Typical Indian Cooking can be quite tedious unless you plan in advance. When you are doing AIP, you have an autoimmune disease to begin with which usually means that you have a lot of pain and inflammation. So considering that, a little planning will be key to making your AIP plan successful!

This section includes most frequently used spice blends and curry pastes that can be made in advance thereby making it easier to make a recipe that calls for it.

Ginger garlic paste is the most common ingredient you will see in this book and I highly recommend making it at home. The flavor that this paste alone will give to your food will be well worth the little time you would need to invest in making this.

The AIP Curry powder and AIP Garam Masala are again blends that you could use when you are baking chicken or fish or making one of the curries / stews in this book. It is an easy way to change up the flavor profile of your dish!

Last, but not least, making your own homemade yogurt (dahi) is not only useful but it's also so much better than any store bought ones (even if you find an AIP compliant one)!

Ginger Garlic Paste

Ginger garlic paste is used so often in Indian cooking that it makes sense to make small batches of it periodically. Homemade is always better than store bought and is so easy to make!

Makes about 1/2 cup of paste

Ingredients:

2 whole garlic heads - peeled and cloves separated
2 inch by 1 inch piece of fresh ginger, peeled and roughly chopped
1/4 cup extra virgin olive oil

Method:

Blend all the ingredients in a small food processor jar until you get a smooth paste.

Transfer to an air tight container and keep in the refrigerator for up to 2 weeks.

AIP Curry Powder

An authentic Indian Curry is a complex blend of flavors and no two curries are the same. However, this curry blend can be handy when you want to get some quick curry flavors!

Makes 3 tbsps

Ingredients:

1 tbsp ground cinnamon
1 tbsp ground ginger
1 tbsp turmeric
1 tsp dried curry leaves, powdered (optional)
1/2 tsp asafoetida

Method:

Mix all ingredients in a dry mixing bowl and transfer to an airtight spice jar.

Notes: If you have whole spices, I recommend you use a spice grinder or coffee grinder to grind them individually and then measure individual spices out per the recipe and then mix everything well.

Reintroduction Notes:
You can add 1 tsp cumin and 2 tsp coriander powder (stage 1 reintroductions) for a more rounded flavor.

AIP Garam Masala

Unlike 'Curry powder', Garam masala is a spice blend that is used in most Indian curries!

Makes about 3 tbsps

Ingredients:

2 tbsp ground cinnamon
1 tsp ground cloves
1/2 ground mace
1 tsp ground ginger

Method:

Mix all ingredients in a dry mixing bowl and transfer to an airtight spice jar.

Notes: If you have whole spices, I recommend you use a spice grinder or coffee grinder to grind them individually and then measure individual spices out per the recipe and then mix everything well.

Reintroduction Notes:
You can add 1 tsp cumin and 1/2 tsp black pepper powder (stage 1 reintroductions) for a more authentic tasting garam masala.

Dry Garlic Chutney

This garlic chutney powder is great to sprinkle on roasted or steamed veggies, on grilled meats and even on flatbreads!

Makes about 1/3 cup

Ingredients:

1 tbsp coconut oil
6 large cloves of garlic, peeled and chopped fine
1/2 cup shredded coconut
1/4 tsp sea salt
pinch turmeric
2-3 fresh or dried curry leaves

Method:

Heat a small skillet or pan and add the coconut oil. Add the garlic and stir fry for 1 minute until crisp. Turn heat off and add all the rest of the ingredients and stir to mix.

Transfer the mixture to a small food processor jar and blend for about 20-30 seconds until you get a coarse powder.

Transfer to an air tight jar or container. Store at room temperature for a week or in the refrigerator for a month.

AIP Chaat Masala

Chaat masala is a spice blend that is tangy and refreshing. It can be just sprinkled on top of cooked foods for an additional burst of flavor! I love to add it to salads.

Makes about 2 tbsp

Ingredients:

1 tbsp dry mango powder (Amchur)
2 tsp black salt (Kala Namak)
2 tsp ground ginger

Method:

Mix all ingredients in a dry mixing bowl breaking any lumps and transfer to an airtight spice jar.

Pack a small piece of paper towel inside the jar to absorb any moisture.

Reintroduction Notes:
You can add 1/2 tsp black pepper powder (stage 1 reintroduction) for a spicy kick.

Homemade Coconut Milk

Fresh homemade coconut milk has the best flavor and I love to use this when I make any Indian curry.

Makes about 3 cups

Ingredients:

2 cups fresh or fresh frozen coconut (grated or sliced) or dried shredded coconut
2 1/2 cups hot water (not boiling) in divided portions

Method:

If using frozen coconut, thaw it first at either room temperature or in the microwave for about 30 seconds.

Add the coconut with half of the hot water(about 1 and 1/2 cups) in a food processor or blender for 30 seconds or so. (Make sure to use a large jar with enough room on top or do it in batches to prevent an explosion)

Place a large fine mesh strainer or a nut milk bag over a large bowl. Strain the coconut mixture through this to get coconut milk in the bowl. You can use your hands to squeeze the coconut meat.

Put the squeezed coconut meat back into the blender along with the rest of the warm water (1 cup) and again blend for another 30 sec or so.

Once again pass this mixture through the strainer/nut milk bag. You will get about 3 cups of coconut milk. Pour the extracted coconut milk in a bottle or jar and place in the refrigerator.

Coconut Yogurt (Dahi)

I missed my yogurt the most when I first started AIP since I liked to eat rice with plain yogurt! So I had to come up with a creamy version!

Makes about 1 cup

Ingredients:

1 cup of coconut milk
1 tbsp arrowroot starch
2 probiotic capsules (with out a prebiotic; I like Innate Response Flora brand)

Method:

In a small sauce pan pour the coconut milk. Take 2 tbsp of the coconut milk from the sauce pan and transfer to a small bowl. Add the arrowroot starch to this small bowl and mix using a spoon to form a slurry.

Heat the sauce pan with the coconut milk on low heat. Once the coconut milk gets slightly hot (about 2 mins), pour the arrowroot slurry into it and keeping heat at low, stir mixture continuously. In about two minutes the mixture will start to thicken. Keep stirring and after a minute, turn heat off. Let this thickened coconut mixture cool for about 5 minutes.

Dip a clean finger into the mixture to make sure it is only slightly warm (lukewarm) and not hot. Now carefully empty the contents of the probiotic capsules into the mixture and disperse well into the mixture by mixing with a spoon. Now transfer the still slightly warm mixture into a clean glass jar.

Place the glass jar in a warm place on the kitchen counter or inside the oven putting the oven lights on for 24 hours.

Instant Pot directions:
Cover the jar with its lid or with a kitchen towel and place inside the insert pot of an Instant Pot. Place the lid and press 'Yogurt' setting. Time will appear as 12 hours or 18 hours. Change time manually to 24 hours.

After 24 hours, open the Instant Pot and remove the jar. Open jar and taste the yogurt to see if it has the level of sourness that you desire. If you want to make sour cream, you can continue to keep it in the Instant Pot for 12 more hours and further strain using a cheese cloth or a fine mesh strainer.

After the yogurt or sour cream is formed, transfer container to the refrigerator and store for 2-4 hours for it to set.

For making sour cream:
Keep the yogurt outside for 36-48 hours and further strain using a cheese cloth or a fine mesh strainer.
After the yogurt or sour cream is formed, transfer container to the refrigerator and store for 2-4 hours for it to set.

BREAKFASTS

I wasn't sure about adding this section since on AIP, we do not encourage typical 'breakfast foods' since they are generally heavy on carbs and low on proteins.

However, when I first started AIP, I found it really hard to eat meat for breakfast. Even now, I have it only occasionally. Bone broth, sweet potato pancakes and vegetable smoothies are my friends. I know that many of you may be struggling with similar issues and so I have included options here that you could eat for breakfast. These include modifications of traditional Indian breakfast foods like spinach paratha and poha. However, do try to pair it with a protein or bone broth to make it a complete meal. I also like to have leftover soups for breakfast.

So I hope this section will help you tide over the initial challenges of breakfast and as you become comfortable with AIP, you should be able to eat any AIP meal for breakfast and not necessarily differentiate breakfast from other meals.

Spinach Paratha

Stuffed vegetable Parathas are a common breakfast in India. I love to have these with apple or mango chutney! You can use fresh fenugreek leaves too, instead of spinach in this recipe.

Serves: 2-4

Ingredients:

1 cup cassava flour (Otto's brand)
1 cup packed fresh baby spinach leaves, finely chopped
1/2 tsp turmeric
1/2 tsp sea salt
1 tsp dried fenugreek leaves (optional)
1 tbsp extra virgin olive oil
About 1 1/4 cups very hot water (see directions)
extra 1 - 2 tbsp olive oil as needed for the dough
Avocado oil for pan frying

Method:

In a large mixing bowl, add the cassava flour, the spinach, turmeric, salt, the dried fenugreek (if adding) and the oil.
Place a kettle filled with water on the stove to heat. Let it come to boil and then turn heat off.

Immediately measure 1/2 cup of this hot water and pour it into the bowl carefully. Use a spatula to mix the hot water into the flour and spinach mixture. Then add the rest of the hot water (3/4 cup) mixing continuously with the spatula. Wait for 2-3 minutes to let the mixture cool.

Once the mixture is cool enough to be handled (should be still warm), use your hands to knead the dough and make a smooth dough. Add the additional 1-2 tbsp of olive oil as needed to make the dough smooth (should not be too sticky). Divide the dough into small ping pong sized balls (about 8).

Heat a cast iron or a non stick frying pan. Flatten each dough ball and then using a rolling pin flatten this ball to make a round (about 4 inches diameter).

Once the pan is hot, turn heat to medium and place the rolled out paratha on it. Cook for about 1 minute and then flip to the other side and cook for 1 more minute. Using a spoon apply some of the avocado oil on top and flip again and cook for 30 more seconds.

Repeat this process with all the dough balls. Serve parathas plain or with apple chutney on the side!

Savory Crepes (Uttapam)

These savory uttapams are easy to make and taste great with either coconut chutney or cilantro coconut chutney. You can make these plain also without adding any veggies.

Serves: 2-3

Ingredients:

1/2 cup cassava flour
1/4 cup arrowroot flour
2 tbsp coconut flour
2 tbsp collagen peptides
1/2 tsp sea salt
1/4 cup finely chopped red onions
2 tbsp finely grated carrots (optional)
4-6 fresh curry leaves, finely chopped
2 tbsp finely chopped fresh cilantro leaves
1/2 inch by 1/2 inch piece of fresh ginger, finely chopped (or about 1 tsp grated fresh ginger)
1 1/2 cups water
About 1/4 cup coconut oil or avocado oil for greasing the pan

Method:

Add all the flours, the collagen and the salt to a mixing bowl. Add the onions, curry leaves, cilantro and ginger. Add half of the water and mix using a spoon making sure there are no lumps. Add the rest of the water and mix again until you get a thick batter.

Heat a stainless steel or a cast iron skillet . When the pan is hot, turn heat to medium and add about a tsp of the oil. Use a brush to spread the oil on the entire surface of the pan. Then take a ladle full (about 1/4 cup) of batter and place in the center of the pan. Then working quickly spread the batter in an outward circular motion to form a larger round (about 3 inches diameter and 1/4 inch thick).

Drizzle some more oil on the outer edges of the crepe. Cover the pan with a lid and let cook for about 3 minutes.

Then take lid off and flip the crepe. Let cook again for 2 more minutes. Fold in half and transfer to a dish. Finish making the rest of the crepes the same way.

Serve the uttapams warm with coconut chutney on the side.

Beet and Berries Smoothie Bowl

This is a delicious, creamy and 'nutrient dense' smoothie bowl filled with the goodness of beets, berries and other vegetables and fruits. The addition of coconut milk (fat) and collagen peptides(protein) makes it a balanced breakfast.

Serves: 1

Ingredients:

1 cup fresh or frozen (thawed) mixed berries (strawberries, blueberries, and/or blackberries)
1 celery stalk, chopped
1/4 cup beets peeled and chopped (can be raw or precooked)
1/2 cup zucchini chopped
1/2 of an organic apple, chopped
1/2 of a ripe avocado, scooped out or sliced
1/4 cup coconut milk
1/2 cup room temperature water
2 scoops collagen peptides
For toppings:
banana slices
apple sliced thinly
kiwi slices
fresh or frozen mixed berries

Method:

Add all the ingredients to a blender and blend on medium speed till creamy and fluffy - about 1 minute.

Pour smoothie into a large bowl and decorate with toppings!

‘Coffee’ Latte (Kaapi)

Kaapi is coffee made the southern Indian way using a percolator and with added milk and sugar. This chicory version is pretty good even without the caffeine! Most of the days I have just this for breakfast.

Serves: 1

Ingredients:

1 cup (8 oz) brewed chicory (see method)
1/4 cup coconut milk or coconut cream
1-2 tsp coconut oil
1/2 tsp unflavored gelatin
1 tsp maple syrup

Method:

For brewing chicory:
Pour water into a coffee maker and brew the chicory brew - For every 1 cup of water, add 1 tsp of chicory granules into the coffee filter. Alternatively, you can either use a french press or simply add the chicory to boiling water and let steep for a couple minutes and then strain.

In a large cooking pot or in the hand blender mixing container, pour about 1 cup of chicory brew and add the coconut milk , coconut oil, the maple syrup and the gelatin. Blend using a hand blender for about 30 seconds and blend the mixture till frothy. Enjoy hot.

Reintroduction Notes:
You can make a brew with a mix of organic coffee (coffee on occasional basis is a stage 1 reintroduction) and chicory.

Banana Coconut Pancakes

These pancakes with crispy edges are filled with gooey bananas and shredded coconut! So yum!

Serves: 2 (4-5 pancakes)

Ingredients:

1/2 of a ripe banana, cut into small cubes (about 3/4 cup)
1/4 cup hot water
1/4 tsp sea salt
2 tsp coconut sugar
1/3 cup cassava flour
1/4 cup shredded coconut
1/2 cup water (room temperature)
About 3 tbsp coconut oil for pan frying

Method:

In a medium size mixing bowl, add the banana slices, the hot water, the coconut sugar and salt. Let sit for 5-7 minutes for the banana to soften and for the mixture to cool.

Then add the cassava flour and the shredded coconut and mix. Then add the rest of the water (at room temperature) and mix till all the flour is well mixed. You will still see chunks of banana pieces which is ok!

Heat a stainless steel pan or a cast iron pan for 2 minutes. To the hot pan, add 1 tbsp of coconut oil and turn heat to medium.

Then using a ladle, pour about 1/2 cup of batter into the pan. Slowly spread the batter using the ladle to form a 1/4 inch thick pancake.

Cover with a lid and cook on medium heat for 2 minutes (do not try to flip before that as it will be soft and will break apart). Flip and cook uncovered for another 2 minutes and transfer to a plate.

Sweet Potato Pancakes

This is a western Indian grain free pancake that is eaten during periods of religious fasting when grains are not consumed.

Serves: 2

Ingredients:

1/2 cup tapioca pearls, soaked overnight in water (they should measure about 1 cup after soaking since they swell after soaking)

3/4 cup mashed white sweet potato or regular sweet potato (boiled, peeled and mashed carefully without introducing any water)

1/4 cup water chestnut flour or tiger nut flour (plus 1-2 tbsp more if needed)

1/4 tsp sea salt

About 2 tbsp coconut oil for pan frying

Maple syrup and fresh fruits for serving

Method:

Wash the soaked tapioca pearls in a colander several times until water runs clear. Then strain completely and blot dry using paper towels. Transfer to a large mixing bowl.

Add the mashed sweet potato, water chest nut flour(or tiger nut flour) and the salt also to the bowl.

Mix well using your hands and form a dough. Dough will be slightly sticky which is ok. If its too sticky, add some more chestnut flour. Divide dough into 5 dough balls.

Heat a stainless steel skillet/frying pan on medium heat.

Take one ball at a time and place on a sheet of parchment paper and pat with your hands to form a pancake shape.

Add a tsp of coconut oil to the pan.
Flip the pancake with the parchment sheet onto your palm so that the pancake touches your palm and then peel the parchment carefully from top and place the pancake on the pan.

Cook on medium heat for about 2 minutes. Then flip carefully to the other side and cook again for another 2 minutes. Transfer to a plate.

Finish cooking all pancakes the same way. Serve warm pancakes with a drizzle of maple syrup and / fresh fruits.

Savory Cauliflower Rice with Sweet Potato (Poha)

Poha is a very popular Indian breakfast food made with flattened rice and potatoes mixed with peanuts. This 'AIP' version uses cauliflower rice, white sweet potato and tiger nuts instead and is equally satisfying and delicious!

Serves: 2

Ingredients:

2 tbsp avocado oil or coconut oil
1/4 cup tiger nuts (soaked overnight)
1/2 of a medium red onion, chopped
6-8 fresh curry leaves (or about 1 tbsp dried curry leaves)
1/2 cup white sweet potato peeled and chopped into 1/2 inch by 1/2 inch pieces
1/2 tsp turmeric
1/2 tsp sea salt
pinch asafoetida (optional)
3 cups cauliflower rice (fresh or frozen)
2 tbsp fresh or frozen grated coconut (or dried shredded coconut)
2 tbsp grated carrots
2 tbsp fresh cilantro chopped fine
1 tbsp fresh lemon or lime juice

Method:

Heat a large stainless steel skillet. Add half of the oil and add the tiger nuts. Toast them slowly on low heat for about 2-3 minutes till they turn slightly golden brown.

Transfer the nuts(draining the oil) to a food processor and pulse for a few seconds to get crushed nuts. Keep them aside.

To the same skillet, add the rest of the oil and add the onions and curry leaves. Saute for 2 minutes on medium heat and add the sweet potato, turmeric, salt and asafoetida (if adding).

Stir to mix and cover and cook for 5 minutes on medium heat until the sweet potato is almost cooked. Now add the cauliflower rice and stir to mix. Cover and cook for about 3 minutes until the cauliflower rice is cooked.

Open the lid and add the coconut, carrots, lemon juice and cilantro. Turn heat off and transfer the warm mixture to serving bowls. Sprinkle the crushed tiger nuts on top!

SWEET TREATS

Desserts in a healing diet? Now some people might find that surprising! But based on my own experience and my experience working with clients I can say that being able to give yourself occasional small treats can help folks stay in a program. No one likes to feel deprived and over time, feelings of deprivation can be detrimental to emotional health and can also lead to stress. Stress is one of the biggest factors that impacts autoimmune disease and it can even derail any progress you make on the AIP diet.

This section gives you a variety of treat options that can make you feel special! Even though you may need to make it on your own, you will experience great joy when you are able to enjoy desserts and feel 'normal'! If you have to go to a party at a friend's house, along with your AIP meal, make a dessert to go so that you can have something special too when others are gorging up on the typical sugary non AIP desserts!

I am especially proud of this dessert section as I have worked really hard to create these recipes and they make me feel so happy! I have tried to recreate traditional Indian desserts like gulab jamun, carrot halwa and kheer because I missed them! I also tried to create new desserts that are a fusion of Indian and American for example Mango Pie, Naan Khatai Cookies and Fried Dough Diamonds. The 'sticky mango rice' is inspired by a similar Thai dessert!

Mango Pie

Mango Pie is a dessert that I have been making for a very long time so I absolutely needed to make a dairy free and grain free version! This crust tastes like a graham cracker crust!

Serves: 6-8

Ingredients:

For the crust:
1/4 cup coconut flour
1/4 cup arrowroot flour
1/4 tsp sea salt
1/4 tsp baking soda
1 tbsp maple syrup
3 tbsp palm shortening, melted
1/2 tsp vanilla extract
For the filling:
2 cups fresh or frozen (thawed) mango pieces, pureed
1 cup coconut milk, unsweetened (I like Aroy-D brand)
1 tbsp grass fed gelatin
1/4 cup water
pinch sea salt
1 tbsp maple syrup
1/8 tsp ground turmeric

Method:

For the crust:
Mix the flours, the salt and the baking soda in a bowl. Then add the maple syrup, the palm shortening and the vanilla.
Mix all together well using your hands. The dough will be crumbly.

Pre heat oven to 350 F. Line a baking tray with parchment paper and spread the crumbly dough on it in a thin layer. Bake at 350 F for 6-7 minutes until golden brown.

Remove from the oven and keep aside to cool. Put the baked crumbs into a Ziploc bag and roll a rolling pin over the bag to get a mix of fine and coarse crumbs. Keep aside.

For the filling:
Line a 6 inch or 8 inch springform pan with parchment paper on the bottom and grease the bottom and the sides with coconut oil.
Pour the coconut milk in a sauce pan and place on low heat.

In a small bowl take the water and sprinkle the gelatin on top of it to get the gelatin wet completely. Let it sit for 5 minutes. Then mix the gelatin with the water – it should form a gel like mixture.

Add this gel to the warm coconut milk and stir hard to dissolve the gelatin completely. Add the salt, the maple syrup and the turmeric. Mix well and turn heat off. Let cool for 5-10 minutes.

Once the coconut mixture is cooled off, add it to a blender and add the mango puree too. Blend till you get a creamy blend.

Pour the mango filling into the prepared pan. Place the pan in the refrigerator for 6-8 hours to set.

Just before serving, spread the cookie crumbs on top of the now 'set' mango mixture and carefully get the pie out of the springform by releasing the base.

Alternately, you can also make this pie as mini pies in ramekins. Pour the filling into 4 greased ramekins. And just before serving, place cookie crumbs on top!

Gulab Jamun

Gulab means 'rose' and gulab jamun means rose flavored balls! These delicious balls made from milk cheese are an absolute must at every major celebration. My dairy free, AIP version is no less in deliciousness!

Serves: 4-6

Ingredients:

1/2 of a large white sweet potato, boiled, peeled and mashed (1/2 cup mashed)
1/4 cup cassava flour
1/4 cup tigernut flour
1/8 tsp sea salt
1/4 tsp baking soda
2 tbsp coconut milk
1 tsp apple cider vinegar
About 1 1/2 cups of avocado oil or palm shortening for deep frying

For the syrup:
1 1/2 cups water
1/4 cup maple syrup
2 tbsp honey
8-10 organic dried rose petals (or 1 tsp rose water)

Method:

In a large mixing bowl, add the mashed white sweet potato.
In a plate, add the cassava flour, tigernut flour, salt, and the baking soda. Mix using a fork to blend.

Add the flour mixture to the bowl with the mashed sweet potato. Add the coconut milk and apple cider vinegar and mix using a spoon until a dough begins to form. Then start to mix using your hands until a smooth dough begins to form. Dough should be moist but not sticky. Divide dough into 10-12 equal shaped balls. Cover the balls with a slightly wet dish cloth to keep them moist.

Heat the oil for deep frying in a small deep frying pan. When hot, deep fry the balls in batches for 3-4 minutes until they turn golden brown on the outside. Transfer to a paper towel lined dish.

In a small sauce pan add all the syrup ingredients and heat the pan for about 8-10 minutes until 1/4 of the water evaporates. Now drop the fried balls into this syrup carefully.

Then turn the heat off and cover with a lid. Let stay covered for about 5 minutes. After that, gulab jamuns can be served either warm or refrigerated and served cold.

Vermicelli Pudding (Kheer)

Kheer is a traditional Indian pudding usually made with rice or with vermicelli. This version with the sweet potato noodles turned out perfect.

Serves: 4-6

Ingredients:

1 cup dried sweet potato noodles, cooked, drained and washed in cold water (Assi Brand)
2 cups coconut milk whole fat, unsweetened
3 tbsp maple syrup
1/8 tsp sea salt
2 tsp arrowroot starch
2 tbsps additional coconut milk
About 15-20 strands of saffron

Reintroduction Notes:
You can add a handful of toasted chopped cashewnuts and almonds (both are stage 2 reintroductions) as a topping.

Method:

Take the cooked and cooled noodles and cut them into about 1 inch long pieces using kitchen shears. Transfer to a sauce pan. Add the coconut milk, maple syrup and sea salt to the pan too. Heat the pan on low heat for a couple minutes.

In a small bowl or cup, mix the arrowroot starch in the additional coconut milk to form a slurry. Slowly add the above mixture to the sauce pan using one hand while stirring the mixture in the sauce pan continuously using the other hand.

Let cook for about 2 minutes and continue stirring until the mixture begins to thicken. Keep stirring and cook for another couple minutes.

Then add the saffron strands into the pan and stir for one more minute. Turn heat off.
Serve pudding either warm or cold. Place in refrigerator for at least 1 hour if serving cold.

Pudding thickens further upon cooling. If it becomes too thick, you can mix a bit of coconut milk to get the desired consistency.

Fruit Salad with Custard

This dessert was my mom's special dessert and she always made it whenever we had guests. The creamy custard along with an assortment of fruits is a perfect way to end a great meal!

Serves: 4

Ingredients:

1 cup coconut milk
1/8 tsp sea salt
1 tbsp maple syrup
1 tbsp arrowroot flour
1 tsp tapioca flour
2 tbsp coconut milk
1/2 tsp vanilla extract
1-2 drops of rose extract or rose water (optional)
2 tbsp collagen peptides

Fruit toppings:
1 cup mix of chopped fruits of your choice (I usually use a combination of any of the following fruits - apple, banana, peaches, pineapple, mango, strawberry, orange and kiwi)
1 tbsp chopped dates
1 tbsp chopped apricots

Method:

In a small sauce pan, add the 1 cup coconut milk and heat on medium heat. Add the salt and maple syrup. As the milk begins to bubble, lower heat. In a small bowl, add the arrowroot flour, tapioca flour and the 2 tbsp water. Mix using a spoon to form a slurry.

Add this slurry slowly into the saucepan stirring the coconut milk mixture using your other hand. Continue stirring on low heat until you get a thick creamy consistency. Turn heat off. Add the vanilla and rose water/extract (if adding). Let cool for about 15 minutes.

Once cooled, add the collagen peptides and mix thoroughly to blend. Store this custard in the refrigerator until serving.

For the topping:
Chop the fruits and keep them in a separate bowl in the refrigerator until serving.

For serving the fruit salad:
In a serving bowl, add some of the custard. Then place some of the chopped fruits and dried fruits on top!

Carrot Halwa

Carrot halwa is another dish that is a 'labor of love' as it needs to be cooked slowly for a long period of time. However, it is absolutely worth the effort!

Serves: 4-6

Ingredients:

3 cups grated carrots (about 3 large carrots)
1 1/2 tbsp coconut oil
1/4 cup coconut chips or coconut flakes
1 can coconut milk
1/4 tsp sea salt
1 cup plus 1/4 cup shredded coconut (divided)
1/4 cup maple syrup
1 tsp ground mace
1 tsp ground cinnamon

Method:

Regular Cooking Pot:
In a wide bottomed cooking pot, add the coconut oil and saute coconut chips for 1-2 minutes stirring frequently until golden brown. Remove using a slotted spoon. Keep aside.

Then add 1 more tbsp coconut oil and add the grated carrots, coconut milk and sea salt. Cover and cook on low heat for 15 minutes.

Open the lid and add 1 cup of the shredded coconut, maple syrup and the spices. Stir to mix and then continue to cook on low heat stirring frequently for about 15-20 minutes total depending upon final consistency desired (not much water left and thick porridge like consistency is achieved).

Stir frequently to avoid scorching at the bottom. When done, add back the toasted coconut chips or flakes and the rest of the shredded coconut.
Serve warm!

Instant Pot:
Press saute on the Instant Pot. Add the coconut oil and saute coconut chips for 1-2 minutes stirring frequently until golden brown. Remove using a slotted spoon. Keep aside.

Then add 1 more tbsp coconut oil and add the grated carrots, coconut milk and sea salt. Pressure cook for 5 minutes. Let pressure release naturally and then open lid.

Press Cancel button and then Turn saute mode on. Change saute setting till you get low saute. Add 1 cup of the shredded coconut, maple syrup and the spices.

Stir to mix and then leave on low saute mode for about 15-20 minutes total depending upon final consistency desired (not much water left and thick porridge like consistency is achieved).

Stir frequently while on saute mode to avoid scorching at the bottom. When done, add the toasted nuts(if adding), the coconut chips and 1/4 cup more of the shredded coconut.
Serve warm!

Reintroduction Notes:
You can add a handful of toasted chopped cashewnuts and almonds (both are stage 2 reintroductions) as a topping.

Naan Khatai Cookies

Naan Khatai cookies are a traditional Indian cookie that are soft, buttery and melt-in-mouth. I must have tried and tested at least 5 different recipes before I was finally satisfied with the result!

Serves: 3-6 (makes 6 cookies)

Ingredients:

1/4 cup arrowroot flour
2 tbsp cassava flour
2 tbsp tapioca flour / starch
⅛ tsp sea salt
⅛ tsp baking soda
3 tbsp softened palm shortening
1 tbsp maple syrup
1/2 tsp vanilla extract

Method:

Pre heat the oven to 350 F.
In a dry mixing bowl, add all the flours, the salt and the baking soda. Mix using a fork to blend everything well. Then add the palm shortening, maple syrup and vanilla. Stir using a spoon to mix. Then use your hands to gently massage the palm shortening into the flour until the flour gets moist and you get a dough. Do not overwork the dough.

Divide the dough into 6 equal sized balls. Take each dough ball and press it flat between your palms until you get a flat cookie (about 1 1/2 inches diameter). The cookie should be thicker in the center as compared to the edges.

Lay the cookies on a baking tray lined with parchment paper. Bake at 350 F for about 14-15 minutes until the bottoms turn slightly golden. (The cookies will appear very soft but they will harden upon cooling).

Take the tray out of the oven and let the cookies cool for about 10-15 minutes before serving.

Fried Dough Diamonds

This snack is like a cookie but it is deep fried and so a bit like deep fried bread. These taste amazing when warm! I find it hard to stop eating them so please make a small batch if you don't want a carb load!

Serves: 2-4

Ingredients:

1/4 cup palm shortening, melted
2 tbsp maple syrup (you can add more if you like, see notes)
1/4 cup coconut milk
1/4 cup hot water
1/4 tsp vanilla extract or vanilla powder
1/4 tsp sea salt
3/4 cups cassava flour
About 1 1/2 cups palm shortening or avocado oil for deep frying
powdered coconut sugar (optional)

Method:

In a large mixing bowl add the palm shortening, maple syrup, coconut milk, the hot water, vanilla and the sea salt. Stir to mix and then add the cassava flour and mix well using a spatula until all the flour is wet.

Then using your hands knead gently to form a dough. (Do not knead too much). Divide dough into 2 equal size balls.

Heat the oil in a small deep frying pot/pan. When the oil is hot, turn heat to medium. Roll each ball between two parchment paper sheets until 1/4 inch thick. Then using a pizza cutter or a knife, make horizontal and vertical cuts on the round piece of dough to get diamond pieces or use a diamond shaped cookie cutter.

Drop the diamond shapes into the hot oil and deep fry on medium heat for about 2 minutes until they puff up and turn golden brown and crisp. Remove from the fryer and transfer to a plate.

Repeat making diamonds from the rest of the dough and deep fry them the same way as above.

You can serve the diamonds immediately or transfer to an air-tight tin/jar and place at room temperature for 4-5 days. You can sprinkle with powdered coconut sugar just before serving.

Notes: You can increase quantity of maple syrup to 3 tbsp or more if you would like the fried dough sweeter. I like it less sweet and occasionally will sprinkle coconut sugar on top.

Plantain Fritters

These yummy crispy fritters with the sweet deliciousness of plantains are a real treat for the whole family! Soft plantains with yellow or black skin are the best for this recipe.

Serves: 2-4

Ingredients:

2 ripe plantains
1/4 cup cassava flour
1/8 tsp sea salt
1/8 tsp turmeric
1/2 cup water
About 1/4 cup coconut oil for shallow frying

Method:

Peel the plantains and cut each one into half horizontally. Then cut each half vertically into 2 first and then again cut each of the quarters further so that you get about 1/2 inch thick slices (you will get 8 pieces from 1 plantain so a total of 16 slices)

In a large mixing bowl add the cassava flour, salt and the turmeric and then add half the water first and stir using a fork to mix and make sure there are no lumps. Then add the rest of the water till you have a slurry. This will thicken slightly upon standing so don't worry if it looks too thin.

Heat a frying pan and add about 2 tbsp of the coconut oil. When hot, slowly dip each plantain slice into the batter and place carefully onto the pan. Don't overcrowd the pan as then you will have trouble flipping the slices.

Cook for about 2 minutes on medium heat and then flip and cook for another 2 minutes until crispy and golden brown. Transfer to a plate. Finish frying all the slices this way. Serve warm!

Coconut Ladoo

'Ladoo' is a traditional Indian sweet shaped as balls and there are lots of varieties. I made these delicious coconut ladoos for Diwali one time and turns out they are perfect as a snack or a treat!

Serves: 4

Ingredients:

1/4 cup water
1 tbsp grass fed gelatin
2 tbsp coconut milk
2 tbsp maple syrup or honey
1/4 tsp sea salt
1/2 cup coconut flour
1/2 cup shredded coconut
1/4 tsp alcohol free vanilla extract or rose extract or crushed dried rose petals
extra shredded coconut for rolling

Method:

In a small bowl, add the water and then sprinkle the gelatin on top of the water slowly until all the gelatin is wet. Use a fork to further mix and wet the gelatin. Keep aside.

In a small saucepan, add the coconut milk and maple syrup and heat on very low flame. Then add the bloomed gelatin mixture to this and stir continuously while on low heat until all the gelatin gets completely dissolved in the mixture. Now add the salt and turn heat off.

To the above mixture, add the coconut flour, shredded coconut and vanilla (or rose) extract. Mix using a spoon and then using your hands, form small balls (8-10.)

Roll each ball in shredded coconut and place on a plate. Place the balls in the refrigerator for about 1 hour to set.

Atte Ka Halwa

There is no equivalent of any western dessert that I can compare this dish to. Atta means flour and in this dessert wheat flour is fried in fat and then cooked in milk to yield a fudge kind of delicious grainy semi solid pudding. This is to die for!

Serves: 2-4

Ingredients:

1/2 cup cassava flour
1/4 cup tiger nut flour
1/4 tsp sea salt
1/2 cup palm shortening (melted) or coconut oil
1/4 cup coconut sugar
1/2 cup boiling water

Method:

In a large wok style pan or a large frying pan, add the cassava flour and roast on low flame for 7-8 minutes stirring continuously until it turns light brown in color (take care not to burn the flour). Add the tiger nut flour and the salt and again stir fry for 1 more minute.

Turn heat to very low and add the palm shortening or coconut oil and stir fry for 2-3 minutes until small lumps form. Then add the coconut sugar and the boiling water and again stir continuously for about 2 minutes or so until all the water evaporates and you get a crumbly but moist mixture. Turn heat off. Serve halwa warm!

Alternatively, you can pour the hot mixture into a greased pan and pat it using a greased spoon. Then transfer the pan to the refrigerator to cool for about an hour. Once cool, you can cut fudge into squares.

Reintroduction Notes:
You can add a handful of toasted chopped cashewnuts and almonds (both are stage 2 reintroductions) as a topping.

Sticky Mango Rice

I fell in love with 'sticky mango rice' dessert the first time I ate it at a Thai restaurant. And I was super elated when I made an AIP version!

Serves: 2

Ingredients:

1/2 cup tapioca pearls (sabudana or sago), soaked in water overnight (or at least for 2 hours)
1/2 cup water
1/4 tsp sea salt
1 cup coconut milk
1 tbsp shredded coconut
1 tbsp maple syrup or honey
1/2 cup fresh or frozen mango pieces, chopped

Method:

Drain the tapioca pearls using a strainer. Wash thoroughly in running water while in strainer.

Place the tapioca pearls in a medium cooking pot and add the water and salt and cook for 2 minutes covered on low heat. Open the lid and stir and add the coconut milk and the maple syrup and shredded coconut.

Cook on medium heat for about 2 - 3 more minutes stirring continuously until all the pearls turn translucent. Turn heat off. Let cool for a few minutes and place in refrigerator for at least 30 minutes before serving.

In a tall serving glass, place alternate layers of this tapioca pudding and the mango pieces and serve! Alternatively, you can serve the pudding in a bowl adding the mango pieces on top.

Crepes with Coconut Filling

These crepes are a comforting treat for me. They are traditionally eaten at breakfast or as a snack with afternoon tea. Maple syrup works as a sweetener as well as to give the filling a delicious flavor!

Serves: 2

Ingredients:

1/4 cup cassava flour
1 tbsp arrowroot flour
1 tbsp coconut flour
1/8 tsp sea salt
1 tbsp coconut milk
3/4 cup water
About 1/4 cup coconut oil for pan frying

For the filling:
1 cup fresh frozen grated coconut (thawed) or shredded coconut (if using shredded coconut mix it with 1 tbsp water)
2 tbsp maple syrup

Method:

Add all the ingredients to a mixing bowl and stir with a spoon to form a thick batter. Heat a stainless steel skillet on medium heat. Add a tbsp of coconut oil to the pan. Then pour a ladle full of batter. Swirl the skillet to form a round shape. Add a tsp more oil on the edges of the crepe.

Cover and cook for 2 minutes. Then flip it and cook for 1 more minute. Transfer to a plate. Finish cooking all the crepes this way. Keep aside.

To make filling:
To the same skillet or another one, add the coconut and the maple syrup. Cook on low heat for about 3 to 4 minutes stirring constantly until the coconut is lightly toasted.

To assemble the crepes:
In a serving plate, place one crepe. Add 2 tbsp of filling in ⅓ section of the crepe. Then start rolling the crepe from that side onwards (like a carpet) until you reach the other end. Repeat for all crepes. You might have some extra filling left which you can serve on the side!

Reintroduction Notes:
You can add 1/2 tsp of crushed or powdered cardamom (stage 1 reintroduction) to the filling for an additional burst of flavor.

Saffron Ice Cream (Kesar Kulfi)

Kulfi is Indian Ice Cream which is made without eggs. Kesar Pista Kulfi with saffron and pistachios used to be my favorite flavor. So I created this AIP version using saffron which tastes pretty amazing!

Ingredients:

2 cups full fat coconut milk (I like the Aroy-D brand)
2 tbsp arrowroot starch
1/4 cup coconut milk
1/4 tsp sea salt
1/4 cup maple syrup
1/2 tsp saffron strands

Method:

Place the coconut milk in a sauce pan and heat on low heat. Mix the arrowroot starch with the rest of the coconut milk in a small bowl and add to the warm coconut milk stirring continuously until the mixture begins to turn thick (about 2 minutes).

Continue to stir and cook for 1 more minute and then turn the heat off. Add the salt, maple syrup and the saffron and stir again to mix.

Let cool for 10 minutes and then pour into a freezer proof container and place in the freezer for 2 hours. Then take the container out and get the contents into a food processor and process until you get a soft churn consistency.

Transfer the mixture back into the freezer proof container and place in the freezer for at least 6-8 hours before serving. Thaw for at least 10 minutes on the kitchen counter before serving.

Note: You can also use an ice cream maker and follow the directions of the manufacturer.

SAMPLE MEAL PLANS AND MENUS

SAMPLE MEAL PLAN 1

	Sunday	Monday	Tuesday
Breakfast	Banana Coconut Pancakes (p239); Pre-Soaked Tiger Nuts	Bone Broth (p88) with a Bowl of Steamed Vegetables	Poha (p243)
Lunch	Vegetable Coconut Stew (p178), Pan Fried Fish (p61)	Chicken Kofta Bowl (p155)	Pan Fried Fish (p61), Salad
Dinner	Shahi Chicken Kofta Curry (p136), Cassava Chapatis (p159)	Vegetable Coconut Stew (p178), Pan Fried Fish (p61)	Turmeric Lemon Chicken (p119), Kale with Coconut (p182)

Wednesday	Thursday	Friday	Saturday
Bone Broth (p88) with a Bowl of Berries and Fruits	Poha (p243)	Bone Broth (p88) with a Bowl of Steamed Vegetables	Banana Coconut Pancakes (p239); Pre-Soaked Tiger Nuts
Turmeric Lemon Chicken (p119) with Salad	Chicken Kofta Bowl (p155)	Chicken and Vegetable Stew (p127)	Fish Molee (p143), Cauliflower Rice
Vegetable Coconut Stew (p178), Pan Fried Fish (p61)	Chicken and Vegetable Stew (p127)	Fish Molee (p143), Cauliflower Rice	Chicken and Vegetable Stew (p127)

SAMPLE MEAL PLAN 2

	Sunday	Monday	Tuesday
Breakfast	Spinach Paratha (p230); Bone Broth (p88)	Chicken Liver Masala (p58) Lettuce Wraps	Spinach Paratha (p230); Bone Broth (p88)
Lunch	Tangy Fish Curry (p132), Mashed Cassava (p185)	Chicken Biryani (p70)	Tangy Fish Curry (p132), Mashed Cassava (p185)
Dinner	Chicken Biryani (p70)	Baked Flounder with Mint Chutney (p115)	Tandoori Chicken Pizza (p80)

Wednesday	Thursday	Friday	Saturday
Chicken Liver Masala (p58) Lettuce Wraps	Spinach Paratha (p230); Bone Broth (p88)	Chicken Liver Masala (p58) Lettuce Wraps	Savory Crepes (Uttapam) (p233) with Coconut Chutney (p204)
Tandoori Chicken Pizza (p80)	Tangy Fish Curry (p132), Cauliflower Rice	Cauliflower and Carrot Soup (p92); Pan Fried Fish (p.61)	BBQ Chicken (120); Salad
Baked Flounder with Mint Chutney (p115)	Cauliflower and Carrot Soup (p92); Pan Fried Fish (p.61)	BBQ Chicken (120); Salad	Cauliflower and Carrot Soup (p92); Pan Fried Fish (p.61)

SAMPLE MEAL PLAN 3

	Sunday	Monday	Tuesday
Breakfast	Sweet Potato Pancakes (p240)	Sweet Potato Pancakes (p240)	Chicken Shaami Kebabs (p45), Sauteed Vegetables
Lunch	Shrimp Tacos (p74)	Shrimp Tacos (p74)	Tuna Chaat Lettuce Wraps (p77)
Dinner	Fish Tikka Masala (p128), Cassava Rotis (p159)	Fish Curry Chowder (p73)	Fish Tikka Masala (p128), Cauliflower Rice

Wednesday	Thursday	Friday	Saturday
Bone Broth (p88) with a Bowl of Steamed Vegetables	Chicken Shaami Kebabs (p45), Sauteed Vegetables	Bone Broth (p88) with a Bowl of Steamed Vegetables	Banana Coconut Pancakes (p239) and 'Coffee' Latte (p237)
Fish Curry Chowder (p73)	Fish Bhurji (p66), Yogurt Rice (p198)	Tuna Chaat Lettuce Wraps (p77)	Broccoli Sprouts Salad (p216), Pan Fried Fish (p61)
Fish Bhurji (p66), Yogurt Rice (p198)	Fish Tikka Masala (p128), Cauliflower Rice	Chicken Dumpling Soup (p96)	Chicken Dumpling Soup (p96)

SAMPLE MEAL PLAN 4

	Sunday	Monday	Tuesday
Breakfast	Chicken Dumpling Soup (p96)	'Coffee' Latte (p237) and a Bowl of Fruits and Tiger Nuts	Bone Broth (p88) with a Bowl of Steamed Vegetables
Lunch	Lentil Soup (p100), Sardine Cutlets (p38)	Lentil Soup (p100), Sardine Cutlets (p38)	Kerala Beef Bowl (p152)
Dinner	Kerala Beef Bowl (p152)	Tangy Fish Curry (p132), Boiled Cassava or Mashed Cassava (p185)	Cod Lemon 'Rice' (p69)

Wednesday	Thursday	Friday	Saturday
'Coffee' Latte (p237) and a Bowl of Fruits and Tiger Nuts	Bone Broth (p88) with a Bowl of Steamed Vegetables	'Coffee' Latte (p237) and a Bowl of Fruits and Tiger Nuts	Beet and Berry Smoothie Bowl (p234)
Cod Lemon 'Rice' (p69)	Lentil Soup (p100), Sardine Cutlets (p38)	Kerala Beef Bowl (p152)	Butter Chicken (p131), Naans (p164/167)
Tangy Fish Curry (p132), Boiled Cassava or Mashed Cassava (p185)	Tangy Fish Curry (p132), Cassava Rice	Butter Chicken (p131), Naans (p164/167)	Curried Beef with Coconut Chips (p46)

Special Occasion Dinner Menu For 2*

	Seafood Special	Meat	Poultry
Appetizer	Crispy Calamari (p57)	Curried Beef with Coconut Chips (p46)	Crispy Chicken Bites (p37)
Main Course	Shrimp and Vegetable Soup (p95); Cod Lemon 'Rice' (p69)	Pork Vindaloo (p135); Cauliflower Pilaf (p194)	Sri Lankan Chicken Curry (p139); Aloo Gobhi (p177); Naan without Yeast (p164)
Dessert	Sticky Mango Rice (p266)	Gulab Jamun (p249)	Fruit Salad with Custard (p253)

**adjust recipe quantities as needed*

	Special Occasion Dinner Menu For 4-6*			
	Menu 1	Menu 2	Menu 3	Menu 4
Appetizer	Kheema Samosas (p42)	Chicken Paapdi Chaat (p50)	Salmon Kebabs (p108); Grilled Veggies	Fish Pakoras (p34)
Main Course	Shrimp and Vegetable Fried Rice (p82)	Sambhaar Soup (p104); Kale with Coconut (p182)	Chicken Biryani (p70)	Butter Chicken (p131); Naan without Yeast (p164); Cabbage and Pineapple Salad (p217)
Dessert	Carrot Halwa (p254)	Saffron Kulfi (Ice Cream) (p270)	Mango Pie (p246)	Gulab Jamun (p249)

**adjust recipe quantities as needed*

RECIPE INDEX

DHANYAVAAD (Thank You)

I am so thankful to God and for all my family and friends for helping me heal. If it weren't for them, I probably wouldn't have been as well and able as I am now. After I began to get better and put my disease into remission, it had been my goal and my dream to bring this book into fruition. But without the support from the following people, this would not have been possible.

To my husband - Thank you for being the rock in my life. And for pulling me out of the trenches telling me that I could indeed overcome my disease. And thanks for all those numerous dinners and kitchen clean ups so I could finish the book!

To my son - Thank you sweetheart for your patience, creativity and humor in bringing this book to life. I will forever treasure in my heart the countless hours we spent together cooped up in your room editing the heck out of this book! Thank you for the laughs! I could not have done this and stayed sane without you. I cannot imagine working with a designer other than you!

To my darling daughter - Thank you molu for always showing a level of maturity way above that of a 14 year old, so I didn't feel so guilty about not being there for you enough. And thanks for managing my social media while I was immersed in writing the book!

To my dear sisters - Thank you for the constant words of encouragement and for always telling me that I could achieve anything I set my heart on! Everyone needs to have two 'cheerleader' sisters like you two in their lives. I feel so blessed.

To my adorable niece and nephew - Thank you for always believing in me and for motivating me to reach the stars!

I also want to thank my friend, Yrena Friedmann, from the bottom of my heart for pulling me out of depression and helping me connect to God. That was the single most thing that helped my recovery.

I am also forever indebted to all the following AIP leaders who have encouraged and helped me in various ways to publish this book: Dr. Sarah Ballantyne (ThePaleoMom.com), Eileen Laird (PhoenixHelix.com), Angie Alt and Mickey Trescott (AutoimmuneWellness.com). I am especially grateful to Mickey for her valuable guidance regarding different aspects of self-publication.

I am so grateful to my friend Amanda Runnels (Unrefined Junkie.com) for reviewing the manuscript and providing valuable feedback.

I am also thankful to all my friends and family who have encouraged and supported me in different ways throughout this project.

ABOUT THE AUTHOR

Indira Pulliadath is a nutritional therapy practitioner (NTP) and an AIP Certified Coach. She has a Masters in Pharmaceutical Outcomes and Policy from the University of Florida and an MBA in Finance from the University of Connecticut. Before working as a Nutritionist, she worked as a researcher in the health care industry for 15 years in the field of pharmacoeconomics and in data science. She started looking into healing diets five years ago to control her severe and debilitating Rheumatoid Arthritis when medications alone were not enough. Diet and lifestyle changes helped her tremendously to reduce her pain and inflammation which in turn motivated her to switch careers and become a nutritional therapist. She lives in Glastonbury, Connecticut with her husband and two children.

Although she has been living in the US for the last 22 years, a piece of her heart still resides in India. She has always been passionate about cooking, especially Kerala cuisine that she grew up eating. You can find her Indian Inspired Paleo and AIP recipes on her blog at cook2nourish.com.

Youtube:
https://www.youtube.com/c/cook2nourish

Instagram:
https://www.instagram.com/cook2nourish

Facebook:
https://www.facebook.com/cook2nourish

Website:
https://cook2nourish.com

Fort Kochi, Kerala, India

Alappuzha, Kerala, India

INDEX

C